Channels of Power

CHANNELS OF POWER

The Impact of Television on American Politics

AUSTIN RANNEY

An American Enterprise Institute Book

Basic Books, Inc., Publishers   New York

© 1983 American Enterprise Institute for Public Policy Research
Library of Congress Catalog Card Number: 83-70755
ISBN 0-465-00933-6
Printed in the United States of America
Designed by Vincent Torre
10 9 8 7 6 5 4 3 2 1

To Nancy, who knows

Contents

ACKNOWLEDGMENTS ix

Chapter 1
Political Reality in the Television Age 3
What Is Political Reality?
The Advent and Reach of the Television Age
Television as a Source of Political Information
"Reality" and "Mediality"
Presidential Debates as "Medialities"
Conclusion

Chapter 2
Bias in Television News 31
The Meanings of "Bias"
Political Bias
Structural Bias
Conclusion

Chapter 3
Television's Impact on American Political Culture 64
The Information Avalanche
The Fast-Forward Effect
The Way We See Politicians
Television's Impact on Voting Turnout
Conclusion

Chapter 4
Television's Impact on American Politicians 88
Changes in Electoral Politics
Changes in Political Parties
How Politicians Use Television
Conclusion

Contents

Chapter 5
Governing in the Television Age   123
   Television's Compression of Time
   Reducing Options
   Weakening the Coalition Builders
   Shortening Elective Tenures
   Weaker Congressmen and Presidents—
      Stronger Bureaucrats
   Conclusion

Chapter 6
On Balance   156
   New Technology, New Impact?
   Television and the American Political System
   The Consequences
   What To Do and What Not To Do
   Conclusion

NOTES   183
INDEX   199

Acknowledgments

THIS BOOK is a revised and expanded version of the William W. Cook Lectures on American Institutions delivered at the University of Michigan Law School on November 17–19, 1981. It is a distinguished series, and I was honored by the invitation to join it. Whatever trepidations I may have felt about addressing an audience of legal scholars were calmed by good advice from my wife, Nancy Boland Ranney, Esq., and by the gracious hospitality with which that great university and law school receive their guests.

My wife and I are especially indebted to Dean Terrance Sandalow and his colleagues for their many kindnesses during our days on the campus. We are also grateful to Professor Samuel H. Barnes and his colleagues in the Department of Political Science for attending the lectures and giving moral support. And it was particularly heartwarming for me to see again after so many years James Donaldson Moore, my high school teacher, coach, and mentor to whom I owe far more than words can ever repay.

I am also indebted to a number of friends and colleagues for helping me to convert the lectures into this book. Albert R. Hunt of the *Wall Street Journal* and PBS's "Washington Week in Review," Thomas E. Mann of the American Political Science Association, Percy H. Tannenbaum of the University of California, Berkeley, Judy Woodruff of NBC News, and Evron M. Kirkpatrick, Michael Novak, and Norman J. Ornstein of the American Enterprise Institute all read parts of the manuscript and made many helpful suggestions. I accepted most of them and probably should have used them all. Certainly they helped to give the book whatever merit it has, and they are

Acknowledgments

blameless for whatever errors of fact and interpretation remain.

President William J. Baroody, Jr. and Vice-President Tait Trussell of the American Enterprise Institute provided support and encouragement. And Randa H. Murphy, as so often in the past, not only protected me from many distractions but transformed my scrawlings into an orderly manuscript.

Finally, the book's dedication is an inadequate way of thanking the person who, more than any other, made the book possible. I shall keep trying to think of other ways.

AUSTIN RANNEY
Washington, D.C.
May 1, 1983

Channels of Power

Chapter 1

Political Reality in the Television Age

IN THE SUMMER OF 1981, I took my son and his friend, both fifteen years of age, to Washington, D.C.'s popular tourist attraction, the Smithsonian's Air and Space Museum. We saw many historic exhibits, including the "flying machine" in which the Wright brothers made mankind's first powered flight, the *Spirit of St. Louis* in which Charles Lindbergh made his solo flight across the Atlantic, and the command module of *Apollo XI* that carried Armstrong, Aldrich, and Collins to the moon and back.

After our tour, I asked the boys which sight they had found the most exciting. Without hesitation they replied, "the *Enterprise*"—that is, a model of the fictitious space ship featured in the long-running television series "Star Trek." Somewhat taken aback, I remonstrated, "But you saw a lot of famous *real* airplanes and space ships, and that's only a model of a stage set for a TV show." My son explained, "Look, Dad, most of the things we've seen here we've already seen on TV. We've both been watching "Star Trek" ever since we were little kids, and the *Enterprise* is just as real to us as all the other things in this museum, and more exciting."

That ended the discussion, but it set me to musing about just what is "real" and what is not in a world in which most American children begin watching television at the age of three months and, by the time they finish high school, have spent less than 12,000 hours in front of a teacher and more than 22,000 hours in front of a television set—indeed, a world in which most American adults watch television more than they do anything else except work and sleep.[1]

My professional concerns soon turned my musings to that particular slice of reality called "politics," and I began to ponder what has become the central topic of this chapter: namely, what is political reality in the 1980s, how do people find out about it, and what difference does the way they find out about it make for the American way of politics? My brief (and losing) exchange with my son called to mind a rather startling story about political reality in the television age that I first encountered in reading a biography of Lyndon Johnson.

As several chroniclers have told it, the story is this. In early 1968, after five years of steadily increasing American commitment of troops and arms to the war in Vietnam, President Johnson was still holding fast to the policy that the war could and must be won. However, his favorite television newsman, CBS's Walter Cronkite, became increasingly skeptical about the stream of official statements from Washington and Saigon that claimed we were winning the war. So Cronkite decided to go to Vietnam and see for himself. When he returned, he broadcast a special report to the nation, which Lyndon Johnson watched. Cronkite reported that the war had become a bloody stalemate and that military victory was not in the cards. He concluded: "It is increasingly clear to this reporter

Political Reality in the Television Age

that the only rational way out ... will be to negotiate, not as victors, but as an honorable people who lived up to their pledge to defend democracy, and did the best they could."[2]

On hearing Cronkite's verdict, the president turned to his aides and said, "It's all over." Johnson was a great believer in public opinion polls, and he knew that a recent poll had shown that the American people trusted Walter Cronkite more than any other American to "tell it the way it is." Moreover, Johnson himself liked and respected Cronkite more than any other newsman. As Johnson's aide Bill Moyers put it later, "We always knew ... that Cronkite had more authority with the American people than anyone else. It was Johnson's instinct that Cronkite was it."[3] So if Walter Cronkite thought that the war was hopeless, the American people would think so too, and the only thing left was to wind it down. A few weeks after Cronkite's broadcast Johnson, in a famous broadcast of his own, announced that he was ending the air and naval bombardment in most of Vietnam—and that he would not run for another term as president. As David Halberstam wrote, "It was the first time in history a war had been declared over by an anchorman."[4] That is surely an overstatement; yet the authority of Walter Cronkite, added to the authority of Clark Clifford and other trusted presidential advisors urging Johnson to wind down the war, may well have tipped the balance.

It seems, then, that the war Lyndon Johnson had been seeing was not the war Walter Cronkite saw. Which was the real war? I do not know the answer to that. But in the end the anchorman's view of reality became the view of the President of the United States. If that was the case, it seems appropriate to begin this book by asking, what is political reality in the 1980s, and where does it come from?

What Is Political Reality?

POLITICAL "COGNITIVE MAPS"

Political behavior, like all human behavior, is guided and shaped by what some scholars call "cognitive maps."[5] As scholars use it, the term refers to the fundamental ideas people have about what the world of politics is really like. This includes beliefs about such matters as which persons and organizations really run the government, what motivates them to choose certain policies and reject others, whether they are honest and competent or venal and bumbling, and what influence, if any, ordinary people have on them. Political cognitive maps also include personal beliefs about the more specific and immediate questions that we call "issues": For example, was there truly a world shortage of oil, as Richard Nixon and Jimmy Carter told us; or was it only a hoax perpetrated by the big oil companies to raise prices? Is the Soviet Union really out to dominate the world and install communism everywhere; or is it only trying to preserve its own system against the attacks of its capitalist enemies? Are most of the people on welfare honest and eager to work but, through no fault of their own, unable to find jobs; or are they lazy cheaters who would rather live adequately without working than better with working? We all have our own answers to these and similar questions. Taken together they constitute the political reality that provides the framework in which we behave politically. But where do we get our answers?

BEFORE TELEVISION

Where we find our answers is a question central to understanding politics, and social analysts have been writing about it for a long time. The scholarly literature on this question that

Political Reality in the Television Age

I studied as a graduate student and beginning college teacher was mostly written in the 1940s and early 1950s, a time when newspapers and radio broadcasting were by far the most widely-consumed media of mass communications and television broadcasting was still in its infancy. That literature generally concluded that the mass media had relatively little impact on most people's cognitive maps, which were mainly the product of two other social processes.[6]

One process was called "political socialization," and it consisted of the course of events by which people from early childhood through adolescence into adulthood acquired most of the basic political beliefs and preferences they held the rest of their lives. Those early studies reported that the most important agents of political socialization were parents, siblings, schools, churches, and peer groups—all composed of people with whom the politically developing individual came into frequent face-to-face contact.[7]

The other process was called "the two-step flow of communication," which was widely believed to be the principal means by which most people picked up whatever political information and preferences they acquired as adults. The process was said to work something like this: In step one, the small fraction of adult Americans who were very interested in politics took in quite a lot of the great stream of political facts and opinions pumped out by the mass media, mainly newspapers, radio stations, magazines, movies, and books. Moreover, most of these politically-interested people consumed the outputs of the mass media selectively, that is, they tended to read and listen only to writers and broadcasters with whose political beliefs and preferences they already agreed. In step two, the politically informed and interested minority initiated political discussions with their families, workmates, and friends. Because they knew and cared a lot more about politics than the others, the interested and informed few largely shaped the beliefs and preferences of the apathetic and uninformed many.

Hence they were dubbed "opinion leaders," and they were widely believed to be the main source of most adults' notions about political reality picking up where the agents of political socialization left off.[8]

However adequate these two theories may have been for the times in which they were advanced, most scholars today believe that both have been made largely obsolete by the most important development in American society since the end of the Second World War—the advent of the television age. Before we examine its impact upon the way Americans learn about politics, let us briefly review how the television age came about and how far it has gone.

The Advent and Reach of the Television Age

Although television by the projection of all-electronic scanning was first developed in the 1920s and regular television broadcasting began in the United States in 1941, it did not become a truly mass medium of communication until the 1950s. But when it came, it came with a rush! In 1947, less than 1 percent of American homes had a television receiver, and there were many areas of the country in which no television signal could be received. In 1950, the percentage of homes owning a set rose to 9, and in the next five years it shot up to 65 percent. By 1960, more than 87 percent of American households had sets, and by the 1970s the proportion rose to 95 percent.[9] In the 1980s there is no part of the United States in which some television signal cannot be received. About 98 percent of all American homes have at least one television set and nearly half have two or more sets.[10] Indeed, there are now more television sets in America than there are telephones, bathtubs, and flushing toilets![11]

But how much are those sets turned on, and is anyone

Political Reality in the Television Age

watching? The answers to these questions are, respectively, a lot, and it depends on what you mean by "watching." Evidence from the Nielsen ratings and other audience surveys shows that the average household set is turned on over six hours a day much of the year and over seven hours a day in the cold-weather months.[12] Let me hasten to add, however, that this does *not* mean that most Americans stare at their sets almost continuously when they are not working or sleeping. Edwin Diamond reports an episode which should ease the mind of anyone who fears that that might be the case:

> On . . . Sunday night, February 7, 1971, a power failure occurring on the East Side of Manhattan temporarily knocked out the Empire State Building transmitter used by all the stations on the New York VHF television band. Elsewhere in the New York area electric power was normal—which meant that television sets still functioned, though with blank, soundless screens. Nevertheless, according to the Nielsen audimeters, about a half-million New Yorkers continued to watch the blank screen—or at least left their sets on.[13]

A number of studies have confirmed the fact that many Americans keep their sets on (for who knows what comfort or reassurance) even when they are not watching. For example, some researchers have mounted time-lapse cameras with wide-angle lenses on top of television sets in randomly-selected homes and filmed whatever goes on in front of those sets. They have found that for about one-fifth of the time the people in the room are not watching. One study reported that children "eat, drink, dress and undress, play [and fight] . . . in front of the set" and that adults "eat, drink, sleep, play, argue, fight, and occasionally make love . . . " in front of the set.[14]

It seems, then, that watching television is a rather special kind of activity. As David Littlejohn characterizes it:

> The very nature of our television receivers and our usual locus of viewing forces a distracted, low-intensity response. This is not a

page of clear print to be focused on privately, nor a living stage or commanding screen in a public theatre. It is a small piece of living room (/den/bedroom) furniture. Looking at it, one still sees all the rest of the half-lighted room and takes in yards of peripheral vision. It is generally dull of definition, made up of dots and lines of a mild headachy blur, either bluish-grey or electronic-neon-off-color, utterly unlike print, film, or reality. . . . It is received not in a classroom, study, or communal gathering place, but in one's private lounge. And it is customarily experienced as a domestic social event of the most relaxing, low-energy kind. 'Watching television' in this country is what you do after the day's work is done, when you haven't the energy to read, or go out—the electronic extension of slippers and pipe. It is something to be chatted over, knitted by, read through, eaten and drunk by.[15]

All very true, and it provides a necessary correction to the rather horrifying picture of the typical American slumped hypnotized in front of a television set five or six hours a day soaking up every electronic message from deodorant commercials to presidential addresses. Yet it would also be erroneous to conclude that watching television plays only a trivial part in most Americans' lives and thoughts. As George Comstock points out:

The most obvious contribution of television to American life is the absorption of time that otherwise would be spent differently. By taking time away from other activities, it has changed the character and availability of other options as well as coloring the way each day is lived out in the average home. The attention to the mass media for which television is responsible represents one of the defining characteristics of life in the second half of our century. . . . It would be a mistake . . . to conclude that because television is not often treated as theater performance it is irrelevant to the life lived around it, for the large number of hours that the set is on each day in the average household makes it the framework within which human interaction occurs.[16]

Political Reality in the Television Age

Television as a Source of Political Information

THE "INADVERTENT AUDIENCE"

Comstock's point is particularly well taken, I believe, when we consider the importance of television as a source of people's notions of political reality. To set the point in proper perspective, it is important to bear in mind several contextual facts. For one thing, no matter how much some critics may deplore the sketchiness of television's political coverage, the fact is that television gives considerably more attention to politics than most viewers feel they need or want. Some observers note that television's coverage of politics was minimal up to the mid-1950s but increased markedly in the late 1950s as a way of refurbishing the networks' images as servants of the "public interest, convenience and necessity," which had been badly damaged by the revelations about the rigged and dishonest quiz shows "Twenty Questions" and "The $64,000 Question." Airing more public affairs programming, including expanding national news broadcasts and giving more attention to politics on those broadcasts, seemed a good way of getting back in the critics' (and the Federal Communications Commission's) good graces. The result, however, has been to tell most viewers more about politics than they really want to know. As Michael Schudson comments, "In a sense, journalists are the patrons of political life. To the degree that this is so, the journalism of the national newsweeklies, most large metropolitan newspapers, and the network television news does not mirror the world but constructs one in which the political realm is preeminent."[17]

The fact is that for most Americans politics is still far from being the most interesting and important thing in life. To them politics is usually confusing, boring, repetitious, and, above all, largely irrelevant to the things that really matter in their lives, such as making friends, finding spouses, getting jobs, raising children, and having a good time. Consequently, most Americans simply make no effort to read every day all the stories, editorials, columns, and features on politics that their newspapers print. They typically glance at the headlines and perhaps a lead paragraph or two, and then hasten on to the sports, entertainment, and comic pages. If they have to make any substantial effort to acquire more or better political information, most Americans will not bother. As some social scientists would say, the opportunity costs are just too high.

For most people viewing television, as we have seen, is an undemanding, passive activity. They turn the set on and leave it on. Quite a lot of the time they sit in front of it, but they certainly do not stare raptly at it every minute and swallow whole every message it emits. Audience studies have shown that most viewers give less than a quarter of their viewing time to newscasts and public affairs programs.[18] So it is quite true, as Thomas Patterson observes, that most people who get political information on television get it because they happen to be watching when political information is broadcast. Unlike people who read about politics in newspapers, books, and magazines, they do not get it because they are actively seeking it.[19]

Hence, in Michael Robinson's apt phrase, the television audience for political information and opinions is mostly an "inadvertent audience."[20] They happen to be in front of the set when politically relevant stories or advertisements are broadcast, and it is too much trouble to tune them out. The typical viewers come home from work, turn on their sets, and tune in the local news to check the weather and learn how their favorite teams made out. The local news is followed by the national news, and they leave the sets on while waiting for, or eating, dinner.[21]

Yet the very passivity of most people's viewing may help to make television an important source of political information. When the local and national newscasts mix some political

Political Reality in the Television Age

stories in with the others, as they usually do, the passive and not-very-political viewers in the inadvertent audience do not bother to switch channels. It is less effort to leave the set alone, knowing that in a minute or two the political stuff will be followed by other, more interesting stories. So the viewers absorb some political information even when they do not seek it. But how much do they trust the information that they come by so passively?

TRUST IN TELEVISION NEWS

Ever since the early 1960s, a number of public opinion studies have consistently shown that nearly two-thirds of the American people say that their main source of news is television, with newspapers a distant second, and radio a very distant third. Moreover, more than twice as many people trust what is broadcast on television more than what is reported by newspapers, radio, or magazines. The data shown in table 1.1 are taken from the Roper poll (many other studies report similar findings).

Given the fact that it is so much easier to get news from television than from newspapers, the figures in the first half of table 1.1 are not surprising. But the fact that twice as many people trust the accuracy of television over that of newspapers makes us ask why. I do not know the whole answer to that question, but let me suggest some parts of an answer. The first comes from the fact that several variables affect any communication's power to convince. One variable is the communication's content—does it come across as unabashed one-sided propaganda or as a reasonable and balanced view? Another variable is the nature of the audience—do we already have strongly-held views on the matter or do we know or care little about it? A third variable is how much the message requires of us—does it ask us to do something that has substantial costs, such as spending our money or going out to cast our votes, or

TABLE 1.1

Use of and Trust in News Sources, 1964–1978

"I'd like to ask you where you usually get most of your news about what's going on in the world today?" (more than one answer permitted)

Source of Most News	1964 (%)	1968 (%)	1972 (%)	1976 (%)	1978 (%)
Television	58	59	64	64	67
Newspapers	56	49	50	49	49
Radio	26	25	21	19	20
Magazines	8	7	6	7	5
Other People	5	5	4	5	5
Don't know	3	3	1	—	—

"If you got conflicting or different reports on the same news story from radio, television, the magazines, and the newspapers, which of the four versions would you be most inclined to believe?" (only one answer permitted)

Most Believable	1964 (%)	1968 (%)	1972 (%)	1976 (%)	1978 (%)
Television	41	44	48	51	47
Newspapers	23	21	21	22	23
Radio	8	8	8	7	9
Magazines	10	11	10	9	9
Don't know	18	16	13	11	12

SOURCE: Surveys by the Roper Organization for the Television Information Office, in *Public Opinion,* August/September 1979, p. 30.

does it merely ask us to "hold" one opinion instead of another without stirring from our chairs?

Certainly another important variable is the communicator's persona: The message is more likely to convince us if we know the communicator than if we do not and it is more likely to be convincing if we like and trust the communicator than if we do not. And all communicators, let us remember, communicate not only their messages but themselves as well.

Television communicates messages about its communica-

Political Reality in the Television Age

tors far more richly than do any of the other mass media. We read the words in a newspaper or a book or magazine, but it is usually difficult to get a vivid sense of what kind of person has written those words. Indeed, as Paul Weaver points out:

> Newspaper news adopts an intensely impersonal narrative voice. In part, this means that the reporter, in writing his story, never speaks in the first person, but the matter goes far beyond that. . . . The news story is couched in the extremely narrow and stylized vocabulary which has become standard for all modern news writing; it too helps to expunge any intimation of the reporter's identity and consciousness.[22]

At first glance, one might think that the newspaper story's impersonal tone would make us trust it more than the more personalized television story. But perhaps the fact that we do not feel we know, and therefore cannot trust, the human source of the words on the page weighs more heavily with most of us.

On radio we hear the voice as well as the words, but disembodied voices are quite different from voices issuing from faces and bodies we see. It is worth remembering, in this regard, that in the first presidential campaign debate between John Kennedy and Richard Nixon in 1960, a majority of those who watched it on television thought Kennedy had "won," while a majority of those heard it on radio thought Nixon had "won." Since the television viewers far outnumbered the radio listeners, Kennedy was widely regarded as the overall "winner," and most analysts (including Kennedy and Nixon themselves) believed that Kennedy's "victory" in the first debate was crucial to his narrow electoral victory in November.[23]

Apparently a great deal of the difference had to do with how the two candidates looked. CBS was in charge of the technical arrangements, and Sig Mickelson, the former head of CBS–TV news, describes what happened during and after the debate:

CBS... was soon on the defensive following charges from the Nixon camp that the Nixon staff had been misinformed on light values and the gray scale of the set and that there were problems with the lighting. Newspaper columnists suggested the vice-president had been sabotaged by CBS makeup personnel, since the vice-president had looked pale and gray throughout most of the performance. Kennedy, on the other hand, appeared with a deep tan, probably a hold-over from the time prior to the campaign he had spent on Cape Cod and in Florida. The vice-president had recently been released from a hospital where he had been treated for an infection, and he was naturally pallid in contrast to his ruddy opponent.

It was later discovered that an inferior type of easy-to-apply makeup had been applied to the vice-president by a member of his own staff, thus, if anything, adding to the contrast between the two candidates. It was also soon discovered that the excessive light which upset the carefully achieved balance in the studio derived from the flood lights which had been placed in front of the vice-president by his own television advisers. The light suit he had worn was judged to have been a mistake. The error stemmed in part from misinterpretation of the description of the gray-tone scale of the set.[24]

In short, for most of us an important part of any communication is not only what the communicator says but what kind of human being he or she seems to be. That information is conveyed far more vividly by television's combination of words, voice, and pictures than by the faceless voice of radio or by the faceless and voiceless words of newspapers. Perhaps that explains why most Americans consume more political news from television than from newspapers and why they rely more on the accuracy of what they see on television than on what they read in newspapers. In any event, television newscasts and public affairs programs unquestionably constitute the major source of political reality for most Americans.

But does being a "source" of political reality mean that television merely depicts, more or less faithfully, the reality it finds—or that television in some sense *creates* reality as well

Political Reality in the Television Age

as, or instead of, depicting it? To these difficult questions we now turn.

TELEVISED REALITY AND "REAL REALITY"

From Plato's parable of the shadows in the cave to the riddle of the tree falling out of earshot in the forest, one of the most persistent and difficult of all problems in epistemology has been the question of whether there is a reality out there that truly exists apart from human beings' limited and flawed perceptions of it. (Perhaps the version appropriate for today's classes in logic is: "If a tree falls in a forest but the event is not videotaped or broadcast on the nightly news, has it really happened?")

There are many versions of that question, but the ones that concern us here can be phrased as follows: Is there a "real reality" of what is truly happening in politics that is quite independent, and perhaps quite different, from its portrayal by television and, for that matter, by newspapers, politicians, and political scientists? If so, can we know that "real reality" well enough to be able to measure accurately how well or badly those who describe and explain it are doing their jobs?

Most people and certainly most political scientists, including myself, are much more comfortable in answering "yes" to both questions, although there are plenty of philosophers to tell us that there is no reality other than what fallible human beings like ourselves sense, manipulate in our minds, and talk about.

An "Electric Mirror"? But these are dangerous waters, and I shall hasten on with the safe but not unimportant empirical observation that most of the people who work in television news believe that there is a real political world out there and that they are reporting it as it is, not creating or distorting it. As the political editor for NBC News, Roan Conrad, put it, "From a newsman's point of view, the news is what happens.

17

The news is what somebody says or does. The news is not a reporter's perception or explanation of what happens; *it is simply what happens*."[25]*

Most people in television news would agree. They often say that they are simply holding a mirror up to the political world so that their viewers can see what is really going on. If that is the case, then to attack television news for broadcasting unpleasant stories about the Vietnam War or the Watergate scandals or the probable costs of reforming the social security system is rather like the ancient Greek custom of killing messengers who brought bad news. But is that the case?

The evidence I have seen indicates that the overwhelming majority of the people in television news are doing their best to depict political reality as it is, and they do not try to slant the news so as to advance the cause of any political party, candidate, ideology, or policy. We shall consider the point at some length in chapter 2. Like everyone else in demanding occupations, they do have their goals. And their first and most important goal is to win from their employers and from their fellow newspeople, including both newspaper and television journalists, a solid reputation for ferreting out the important stories and presenting them accurately and tellingly. Achieving this goal can bring great personal and professional fulfillment, higher salaries, better assignments, an occasional Emmy or Peabody, and perhaps even one day the ultimate goal—occupation of the anchor chair of a network's nightly newscast. They may personally and privately prefer particular candidates, causes and parties, but those preferences are clearly far less important to them than their professional success and standing.

It must also be said, however, that sometimes their techniques, to say the least, blur the distinction between the real world and their depiction of it. Edward Jay Epstein, in what I

---

* Emphasis added.

Political Reality in the Television Age

believe to be the best book yet written about television news, cites as an example the case of the widely praised CBS documentary program entitled "Hunger in America," first broadcast in 1968. As Epstein describes it, the hour-long show opened with a film of a baby actually dying as the camera took its picture. He continues:

> Over this scene ... the narrator, Charles Kuralt, said: "Hunger is easy to recognize when it looks like this. The baby is dying of starvation. He was an American. Now he is dead." Millions of viewers naturally assumed that the baby died of starvation, or malnutrition. However, this was not the case. A government investigation subsequently disclosed that the dying baby, whom CBS photographed to illustrate the effects of "starvation," actually was a three-month premature child, weighing less than three pounds at birth, whose parents were neither poor nor starving. The mother, a schoolteacher, had the premature birth after an automobile accident. Thus there was no medical reason to suspect that malnutrition or starvation was in any way connected with the death of the child. In response to criticism on this point, Richard Salant [then president of CBS News] said in a televised interview three years later: "In that area, at that time, and in that hospital, babies were dying of malnutrition." In other words, even though the pictures, with their "tremendous impact," turned out to be of something quite different than they purported to be, the underlying message of the program might still be true.[26]

A "Flashlight in the Attic"? If television news is not quite an "electric mirror," what is it? Some have suggested that a more appropriate metaphor would be that of a flashlight blinking on and off in a dark attic. When it blinks on, its narrow beam reveals the shape of a few of the objects cluttering the attic, but, after allowing for commercials, the national television newscasts are on for only twenty-six minutes each evening, and their quick-on and quick-off images cannot show as much or be studied as much as those of a mirror.

Metaphors aside, the point is that selection and editing, while significant in producing newspapers, are the very es-

19

sence of television news.[27] This is the case, not because television news people are dishonest or eager to slant the news, but because of the basic nature of their medium. Where newspapers have pages of information, television has only paragraphs; and where pictures are add-ons for newspapers, they are at least as important as correspondents' and anchormens' words in television.

Consequently, each network's news producers and editors have to decide, usually well in advance, which few political events out of many possibilities they will cover with their own cameras and crews each day. At each scene those cameras and crews have to choose which of the many happenings available they will actually shoot. Back at the studio the producers and editors have to decide every day what 1 or 2 percent of the thousands of feet of film and videotape their crews have shot they will actually use on that night's newscast. And even though they sometimes get extra time in the form of special newscasts to cover cataclysmic events, such as attempts to assassinate presidents and popes or the seizure of American hostages, they almost never have an equivalent of the extra space newspaper editors can commandeer. About the only time television news teams have that kind of space is on those rare occasions when they are permitted to cover live from beginning to end such top stories as a national party convention or a president's funeral or a royal wedding.

How, then, can television news hope to compete with newspapers as a source of information about politics or anything else? The answer is that television must get the maximum impact from its few minutes, and its producers and editors try to accomplish that by fitting each story into a larger theme and weaving into every account of what happened an explanation of what it means.

Paul Weaver has put the point precisely in describing the

Political Reality in the Television Age

essential differences between newspaper news and television news:

> The standard newspaper news story is organized according to the principle of the "inverted pyramid." Its subject and focus is a single, unitary event as defined in one or two sentences (the headline and lead paragraph). Having stated in the simplest and most reductionist of terms the bare bones of the event (who, what, where, when, and so on), the newspaper news story . . . has already achieved a kind of completeness and can be terminated at that point without rendering it unintelligible. . . . But the news story . . . goes on, in a quasi-random sequence of syntactically crude sentences and disjointed paragraphs, to adduce additional data that elaborate on this or that aspect of the story-, topic-, and event-defining headline and lead. . . . the objective here being to enable an editor to cut as much material as needs to be cut to make the story fit the available space. . . .
>
> The television news story is radically different. Unlike the newspaper news story, which is designed not to be read in its entirety while still achieving intelligibility, the television news story is a whole that is designed to be fully intelligible only when viewed in its entirety. Its focus is therefore upon a theme which runs throughout the story and which develops as the story moves from its beginning to its middle and then to its end. Information, narrative, sound, and pictures are selected and organized to illustrate the theme and to provide the necessary development.[28]

WHERE TELEVISION GETS ITS NEWS

Thus the distinctive thing about television news is not the events it chooses to report but how it reports them. For while selection and editing are important components of newspaper news, they, together with the need for "good visuals," are the main imperatives shaping the presentation of television news.

But how do the networks perform the basic intelligence function of finding out what is going on so that they will know what events to report? The answer is that the enormous expense of taping, editing, and broadcasting television news precludes the networks from gathering much of their own intelligence. "Instead," says Edward Jay Epstein, "for advance notice of news events, the networks rely heavily on the wire services, the *New York Times*, and other secondary sources."[29] Most observers would add to that list a few other highly esteemed newspapers, especially the *Washington Post* and the *Wall Street Journal*, and the newsmagazines *Time* and *Newsweek*.

Typically, the producers, editors, correspondents and anchormen who decide what will appear on the networks' nightly newscasts read closely every day what the wire services and the top newspapers have to say about what has just happened that is important and what is about to happen that will be important. If they have missed any of the just-happened events, they rewrite what the print press says about them and try to add appropriate pictures, often from file footage. And they make advance assignments of their own camera crews and correspondents to get pictures and accounts of what the print press tells them are the important events about to happen.[30] It may be, then, that the old "two-step flow" has been reincarnated in a new form: The wire services and the top newspapers tell the networks what is newsworthy, and the networks pass it on to the mass public.

"Reality" and "Mediality"

Not infrequently an event regarded as newsworthy by the newspapers takes place in such a way that it cannot readily be presented by the pictures, graphics, and voice-over commentaries that constitute the syntax of television. Such events are often transmuted into, or replaced by, the large category of happenings that Daniel Boorstin calls "pseudo-events" and

Political Reality in the Television Age

Michael Robinson calls "medialities."[31] They are events that take place mainly to be shown on television—events that, in the absence of television, would not take place at all or would take place in a different manner.

Some "medialities" are planned and performed by political organizations for the purpose of getting free television exposure for their causes, for example, protest demonstrations, "walkabouts" by political candidates, quickie inspection tours of disaster areas by presidents and governors, and so on. Television news producers are well aware that many organizations try to manipulate them in this way, and if they suspect that an event is being staged solely for their cameras, they may refuse to cover it, unless, that is, they think it will make a good eye-catching item for their newscasts.[32]

Many "medialities" are created or welcomed by the networks for the purpose of ensuring good stories that might otherwise be too costly or difficult to get. As Epstein points out, the networks' technical and economic constraints force them to fill up a good deal of their news time with such events. To produce good newscasts they need good quality pictures of interesting people and actions. To get good quality pictures they need experienced camera crews, good light, not too much extraneous noise, and time to edit the videotapes and add the commentaries. Camera crews are expensive and unwieldy, so the networks maintain their own crews in only a few of the biggest cities. It is therefore highly desirable to schedule them well in advance for events that they believe will yield broadcast-worthy items. Events such as interviews, press conferences, congressional hearings, presidential trips, protest demonstrations, building demolitions, and soldiers firing guns fill the bill every well. Many of these events would probably take place even if they were not covered by television, but their atmosphere and, in many cases, their impact would be very different with no lights and cameras around.[33]

Presidential Debates as "Medialities"

The debates between the presidential candidates in 1960, 1976, and 1980 are instructive for understanding the relationships between televised reality and "real reality." In 1960 the networks wanted to sponsor a series of debates between Richard Nixon and John Kennedy, but could not do so while Section 315 of the Federal Communications Act remained in force. That section of the act required that if a station provided to any candidate for a political office an opportunity to appear on the air, it had to provide equal opportunities to all other candidates for the office, which meant that the ten minor-party presidential candidates would have to have the same amount of prime time as any given to the Kennedy-Nixon debates. So Congress was persuaded to suspend the operation of Section 315 for the two-man debates. Four were held, over 100 million people watched or listened to at least one, and most observers believed that the debates played a key role in Kennedy's eyelash victory over Nixon in November.[34]

In 1964, 1968, and 1972 the favored candidates, Johnson and Nixon, decided that debating would not serve their interests, so there was no serious pressure to suspend or repeal Section 315, and no debates were held. In 1975, however, the Federal Communications Commission ruled that television and radio stations and networks could cover, as bona fide news events, debates between two candidates sponsored by a nonbroadcast organization without having to provide equal time for other candidates for the office. In 1976 the League of Women Voters seized the opportunity and invited President Gerald Ford and his opponent Jimmy Carter to participate in debates the League would sponsor and the networks would cover as news events. Three Carter-Ford debates were held,

Political Reality in the Television Age

and a fourth was added between vice-presidential candidates Walter Mondale and Robert Dole.

Whether the 1976 debates were realities or "medialities" soon became unclear. Toward the end of the first debate, which was watched by over 120 million people, something broke and the sound went dead although the picture continued to be transmitted. Clearly, if the event had been, as officially stated, a debate sponsored by the League for the benefit of the audience in the Philadelphia auditorium with the networks there merely as reporters, the debaters would have gone on as if nothing had happened, and the networks' inability to broadcast their remarks live would have been the networks' tough luck. But that was not what happened. As soon as the audio failed, the proceedings stopped abruptly and remained suspended for the entire embarrassing twenty-six minutes it took the networks to get their sound equipment working again. During this gap, however, the cameras continued to sent out pictures of the two candidates who remained at their podiums, not speaking to each other or to their friends and advisors, but standing motionless in dignified silence. Finally the audio was repaired, the sound went back on the air, and the debate was resumed. Clearly, the audience that mattered was the millions watching on television, not the hundreds present in the hall.

The 1976 debates raised at least one additional question about their status as "reality" or "mediality." This question arose after President Ford's now-famous gaffe in the second debate, in which he said that Poland and the other Eastern European nations were not under Soviet military domination. Polls taken twelve hours after the debate reported that few viewers were put off by Ford's remarks about Eastern Europe, and 53 percent thought that he had won the debate. During the next few days, however, television and the newspapers repeatedly quoted the views of commentators that Ford had committed a terrible boner and that as a result Carter had won. Polls taken later in the week reported that 58 percent of the people now thought that Carter had won and that Ford's statement on Eastern Europe was the main reason.[35]

Here, then, were events that almost certainly would not have taken place if the networks had not covered them. Most viewers drew certain conclusions about the events from their own direct observations of them on television, but many of them changed their minds when the events were interpreted for them by the medias' experts in the days following. In such a situation, any distinction between "real reality" and "televised reality" becomes blurred, to say the least.

However we may classify them, presidential debates of one kind or another nevertheless continued to play important roles at various stages of the 1980 election. For example, John Anderson first attracted national attention by his performance in the televised debate among six Republican hopefuls in Iowa in January, and Ronald Reagan's absence from that debate was widely thought to have cost him his expected victory in the precinct caucuses. A month later, however, Reagan more than recovered by his performance in the Nashua affair: Reagan challenged George Bush to a two-man debate three days before the crucial New Hampshire primary. Bush accepted, but when the time came four other Republican aspirants showed up and asked to be included. With the cameras whirring away, Reagan affably agreed to let them in, while Bush sat stony-faced, insisting on the original agreement to keep it to two participants. It made for great television pictures, and shots of Reagan's and Bush's behavior in Nashua were shown repeatedly in the next three days before the balloting. Many observers believed that the episode was the key to Reagan's come-from-behind win over Bush in the primary.

President Carter, on the other hand, consistently refused Edward Kennedy's repeated challenges to debate during the

Political Reality in the Television Age

Democratic primaries, and Carter's continuing success in those primaries seemed to vindicate his strategy.

In the general election campaign the League of Women Voters again invited the two major candidates to participate in a series of debates, and, after much agonizing about whether to invite John Anderson, now an independent candidate, they finally decided that if Anderson stood at 15 percent or better in the polls by early September they would invite him. He passed the test and got the invitation. However, while Reagan agreed to the debate, Carter stuck to his position that he would participate only in a two-person debate with Reagan. The Anderson-Reagan debate was broadcast live by CBS and NBC, but ABC carried a movie instead. Neither man made any major mistakes, but Anderson failed to make the breakthrough he had hoped for, and his support dwindled thereafter.

As the campaign entered the last three weeks, all the polls showed Reagan leading Carter but with a much larger than usual number of people unenthusiastic about both candidates. As his last major gambit to pull out the election, Carter challenged Reagan to a two-man debate, and in late October Reagan, to many people's surprise, accepted. The debate was held in Cleveland on October 28, just seven days before the election, and this time all three networks carried it live. Afterwards each side claimed that their man had "won," but the polls showed that most people thought Reagan had had the better of it, and many observers believed that the Cleveland debate more than anything else converted a narrow and shaky Reagan lead into the 10-percentage-point margin by which he won the election a week later.[36] For the media buffs, however, perhaps the most memorable event was as pure an example of a "mediality" as we will ever see: ABC, with great fanfare, invited viewers to call in after the debate and report who they thought had won. Despite the fact that a less scientific poll could hardly be imagined, ABC still won a lot of attention for its announcement that Reagan had won by a two-to-one margin.

The presidential debates, then, have provided excellent examples of "medialities." I do not know what their future will be, but I suspect that it will not be decided by what Congress does with Section 315 or what the League of Women Voters does with its plans and invitations. I suspect it will be decided by whether in future elections both candidates will calculate that they stand to gain more than they will lose by debating.[37] In making their decisions they might be well advised to bear in mind these facts: In each of the three preceding sets of debates one participant was the incumbent (or, in the case of Nixon in 1960, a quasi-incumbent); in each case the challenger was generally thought to have won the television debate; in each case the challenger defeated the incumbent in the election; and in each case the challenger's perceived victory in the debate was seen as a key, many would say the key, to winning the election. So in these senses, at least, the political "medialities" created by the presence of television have been at least as important in presidential politics as any "real reality" that we can point to.

In the light of all this, what can we say about the nature of political reality in the television age?

Conclusion

Throughout this chapter I have been using the terms "televised reality" and "real reality" as though they referred to distinct states of affairs and as though "real reality" can and should be the benchmark against which "televised reality" should be measured and judged. Not everyone agrees, however. Political scientists Dan Nimmo and James Combs have written a book

Political Reality in the Television Age

based on the premise that no person's cognitive map of political reality can be based on his or her direct, unmediated experience. Everyone's mental picture of political reality (including, presumably, Nimmo's and Combs's) are, in their words:

> ... not the products of direct involvement but are perceptions focused, filtered, and fantasized by a host of mediators—the press, entertainment programming on television, movies, popular magazines, songs, and group efforts in election campaigns, political movements, religious movements, and government policy making.... Mediated, secondhand reality is one's politics.[38]

Michael Novak, a veteran political campaigner as well as a social theorist, has written in the same vein:

> Anyone who has participated in a large-scale event comes to recognize vividly how strait and narrow is the gate between what has actually happened and what gets on television. For the millions who see the television story, of course, the story is the reality. For those who lived through a strenuous sixteen-hour day on the campaign trail, for example, it is always something of a surprise to see what "made" the television screen—or, more accurately, what the television screen made real. That artificial reality turns out to have more substance for the world at large than the lived sixteen hours. According to the ancient *Maya*, the world of flesh and blood is an illusion. And so it is.[39]

Yet it is hard to abandon completely the idea that there is a "real reality" out there against which "televised reality" should be measured. Nimmo and Combs urge their readers to apply "reality testing" to all the portrayals of political reality by television and the other mediators. And Michael Novak often complains about the inaccuracy, and sometimes about the bias, of what he has heard from Roger Mudd or Dan Rather the night before. So what may be political reality for the "world at large" may not be political reality for people such as Nimmo, Combs, and Novak. They, like the author and many readers of this book, are part of that small minority of Americans for whom politics is endlessly fascinating and who soak up all the political information they can get from all sorts of sources—the *New York Times* and the *Wall Street Journal, Time, Rolling Stone,* the *Nation, Commentary,* books, conversations with friends, active participation in political organizations—and, yes, television newscasts and documentaries, too.

Perhaps the key point was best put in Lee Thayer's remark that "whatever one or more men can and do talk about, but which is not amenable to direct sensory contact by them, has no reality beyond what can [be] and is said about it."[40]

If that is the case, then the question about political reality in America in the 1980s is who says what to whom. Prior to the advent of television in the mid-1950s, as we have seen, most Americans got their notions of political reality mainly from what they were told by those of their families, friends, and workmates who were interested enough in politics to talk about it. But television has overridden the "two-step flow" and bypassed the "opinion leaders." Most of the talk that most Americans now see and hear about politics comes to them in passing as they sit in front of their television sets after the local news and weather forecast have been given and before their favorite "sit-com" or cop show comes on. So for them, if not for the small minority of political buffs, televised political reality *is* "real reality." And that fact, I believe, is crucial for understanding how and why the American way of politics has changed in the television age.

Chapter 2

Bias in Television News

ON NOVEMBER 13, 1969, the vice-president of the United States, Spiro T. Agnew, addressed the Midwest Republican Conference in Des Moines, Iowa—and over a decade later parts of that speech still resonate in some ears.[1] Agnew began by noting that ten days earlier President Richard Nixon had given a nationally televised report on the new administration's policy toward the Vietnam War. Immediately following the talk, each of the three networks, as was their wont, had broadcast commentaries by a battery of its correspondents. As a result, Agnew said, the president's report had been "subjected to instant analysis and querulous criticism . . . by a small band of network commentators and self-appointed analysts, the majority of whom expressed in one way or another their hostility to what he had to say."

This objectionable practice, the vice-president continued, raised the question of whether the American people have a right "to form their own opinions about a presidential address" without having it "characterized through the prejudices of hostile critics before it can even be digested." But it also raised more fundamental questions about the bias of television news and its role in the nation's political life. In Agnew's words:

> Now how it this network news determined? A small group of men, numbering perhaps no more than a dozen anchormen, commentators and executive producers, settle upon the 20 minutes or so of film and commentary that's to reach the public. This selection is made from the 90 to 180 minutes that may be available. Their powers of choice are broad.
> They decide what 40 to 50 million Americans will learn of the day's events in the nation and in the world. . . .
> They can make or break by their coverage and commentary a moratorium on the war.
> They can elevate men from obscurity to national prominence within a week. They can reward some politicians with national exposure and ignore others. . . .
> Nor is their power confined to the substantive. A raised eyebrow, an inflection of the voice, a caustic remark dropped in the middle of a broadcast, can raise doubts in a million minds about the veracity of a public official or the wisdom of a government policy. . . .
> Now what do Americans know of the men who wield this power? . . . We do know that to a man these commentators and producers live and work in the geographical and intellectual confines of Washington, D.C., or New York City. . . . Both communities bask in their own provincialism, their own parochialism. We can deduce that these men read the same newspapers. They draw their political and social views from the same sources. Worse, they talk constantly to one another, thereby providing reinforcement to their shared viewpoints. . . .
> The American people would rightly not tolerate this concentration of power in government. Is it not fair and relevant to question its concentration in the hands of a tiny, enclosed fraternity of privileged men elected by no one and enjoying a monopoly sanctioned and licensed by government?

Bias in Television News

The storm broke immediately. Tens of thousands of people called their local television stations, and two out of three praised Agnew's speech.[2] However, Julian Goodman of NBC issued a statement condemning Agnew's use of his high office "to criticize the way a government-licensed news medium covers the activities of government itself. . . . Evidently he would prefer a different kind of television reporting—one that would be subservient to whatever political group was in authority at the time." And Dr. Frank Stanton of CBS called the speech an "unprecedented attempt by the vice president of the United States to intimidate a mass medium which depends for its existence upon government licenses." Whatever may be the deficiencies of CBS's newsmen, Stanton declared, "they are minor compared to those of a press which would be subservient to the executive power of government."[3]

Most comments at the time fell into one or the other of these two highly partisan modes. But there were some America-watchers, then and now, who regretted that, by raising such important questions in such a partisan and polemical way, Agnew had all but precluded dispassionate discussion of them.

Perhaps in the 1980s, now that both Mr. Agnew and Mr. Nixon have left active political life for their special niches in history, it is possible to raise these questions in a more propitious atmosphere. It seems to me that, at least, Agnew's charges were and remain serious. If television plays as important a role in creating political reality for Americans as I contend in chapter 1, and if that reality is systematically biased in favor of a particular ideology or party or candidate, then one of the most basic preconditions for democratic government does not exist in this land, and those of us who care about that should think hard about how we can induce the broadcasters to maintain a more objective stance without violating their First Amendment rights.

On the assumption, then, that one can raise these topics without in any way appearing to be a supporter of Spiro T. Agnew, in this chapter I propose to deal with three main questions: First, is there systematic and recurring bias in the depiction of politics by television news in America? Second, if so, what kind of bias is it and why is it there? And third, what are its consequences?

The Meanings of Bias

Perhaps the place to begin is to clarify what we mean by "bias" in television news. The first point to note is that failure to "present all the facts" does not, by itself, constitute bias. Every student of human communication knows that it is unavoidably a selective process. No observer can absorb and communicate every fact about any observed situation, and newspaper reporters and television correspondents are no exceptions. Moreover, no newspaper has the space to print everything that its reporters know about all the matters they cover; hence editing (choosing which of the many facts at hand will actually be published in the limited space available and deciding how they will be presented) is at least as essential as reporting for putting out a newspaper. And, as we shall see in detail later, the "newsholes" in television newscasts are much smaller than their newspaper counterparts, and so the editing process is even more central to the way television presents the news than it is to what newspapers do.[4]

As most people use the term, bias in reporting and editing the news means partiality—that is, deliberately shaping the content and presentation of the news so as to advance the cause of a particular party, candidate, or ideology. Doris Graber reports that in one year alone the Federal Communications Commission's Broadcast Bureau received more than

Bias in Television News

100,000 complaints about television programming.[5] Many of these complaints charged the networks with slanting their news reports by such practices as lying (knowingly falsifying the facts), distortion (deliberately overemphasizing some facts and underemphasizing or ignoring others), and imposing their own value judgments (indicating by word or gesture which people, institutions, and actions are good or bad).

Presumably the opposite of bias in this sense would be impartiality—the newscasts would present all the relevant and important facts as they exist, give each fact its proper emphasis, and keep the broadcasters' personal preferences entirely out of the picture, or at least clearly label them as personal preferences.

Certainly these are widely-accepted canons of good journalism, and, as observed in chapter 1, most television newspeople regard themselves as journalists, not as entertainers or personalities. As such, they try their best to live up to their craft's highest standards, and their personal goals of professional success can be achieved only by gaining reputations as good journalists, not as advocates for political causes. Many of them claim that essentially they are simply holding up an "electric mirror" to society that shows it as it is, warts and all. And if Spiro Agnew and other politicians do not like the results, let them pursue the policies and get the results that can accurately be presented as good news.

Political scientist C. Richard Hofstetter makes an important distinction between two kinds of possible bias in television news that will underlie my argument in the rest of this chapter. One kind is political bias. If and when it appears in television news, it can be recognized by the following defining characteristics.

- Its source would be the desire of newspeople to advance a particular political cause—an ideology such as liberalism, a policy such as the Equal Rights Amendment, a party such as the Democrats, or a candidate such as Edward Kennedy.

- Its objects would be to increase the viewers' support for the cause and to stimulate them to do something to advance it.
- Its criteria of success would be such manifestations of increased viewer support as the "right" candidates winning elections, the "right" policies being enacted into law, and the "wrong" policies and candidates being rejected.
- And its vision of political reality would be as a kind of morality drama, with good pitted against evil.

As we shall see in a moment, there are plenty of people who believe that television news is shot through with political bias, although they do not all agree on just what causes the bias favors. But there can be another, quite different kind of tilt in television news that, following Hofstetter, I shall call "structural bias." If and when it appears in television news, it will have these defining characteristics:

- Its source would be the essential nature of television and the organization of television news, the desire of the people in the business to do their jobs according to the medium's established professional standards, and to be paid well and promoted for doing so.
- Its object would be to present the most important stories so as to make them interesting in both pictures and words, to make them meaningful for their viewers, and to do all things better than their competitors do them.
- Its criteria of success include large shares of the television audience, strong budgetary support by the networks, and critical acclaim by the broadcasters' peers and by the print media.
- And its vision of political reality would be a game played by politicians and pressure groups seeking to advance their special interests.

Now let us be clear that a structural bias would be as much a tilt toward a particular way of portraying politics as a political bias would be. But the directions of the tilts would be different and their impact upon the American way of politics would be different.

Some critics have charged television with having a liberal

Bias in Television News

political bias, others have claimed it has a conservative political bias, and still others have argued that it has a structural bias against all politicians, particularly those in power. In the remainder of this chapter I shall examine each of these positions.

Political Bias

A TILT TO THE LEFT?

Spiro Agnew's indictment in his Des Moines speech has also been made by a number of other commentators. They charge that the networks, together with the *New York Times*, the *Washington Post*, and the rest of the liberal press, conduct a deliberate and persistent campaign to win support for the Democratic party and liberal candidates and causes over the Republican party and conservative candidates and causes. After Agnew, the best known exponent of this view has been Edith Efron, notably in her *The News Twisters*[6] and her columns in *TV Guide* magazine.[7]

Efron's case is based on her analysis of what the three networks said about the presidential campaign during the final weeks of 1968. She identified every sentence containing what was, in her judgment, a positive or negative comment about the three presidential candidates, Hubert Humphrey, Richard Nixon, and George Wallace, and about a list of issues important to conservatives. She then totaled the positive and negative statements about each candidate and found that the proportion of unfavorable to favorable opinions was far greater for Nixon than for Humphrey or Wallace. She declared:

> ... There is one conclusion to be drawn from comparison of the opinion aired on Mr. Nixon and Mr. Humphrey: all three networks clearly tried to defeat Mr. Nixon in his campaign for President of

the United States. On the basis of quantitative differences between the Nixon-Humphrey figures alone, no other conclusion is tenable. And the qualitative nature of the opinions chosen for transmission about both men confirms this conclusion.... Network reporters in alliance with Democratic-liberal politicians portrayed Hubert Humphrey as a talkative Democratic saint studded over with every virtue known to man. Deprived of reporters in league with Republican-conservative politicians, Mr. Nixon is not portrayed as a human being at all but is transmogrified into a demon out of the liberal id.... If Richard Nixon is President of the United States today, it is in spite of ABC-TV, CBS-TV, and NBC-TV. Together they broadcast the quantitative equivalent of the *New York Times* lead editorial against him every day—for five days a week for the seven weeks of the campaign period.[8]

Efron next asked why the networks were so biased in favor of Humphrey. There was no mystery about it, she said. Television news is controlled by its producers, editors, reporters, and anchormen, not by the people who own and operate the networks' affiliated local stations. With hardly an exception, the newscasters are upper-middle-class people with Eastern backgrounds and Ivy League educations. They are steeped in the lifestyles and political values of New York, Washington, and Hollywood, and they have only contempt for the lifestyles and values of the rest of the country. Consequently, they are almost all Democrats and left-liberals or radicals. They are proabortion, pro-women's liberation, pro-black militants; and they are antibusiness, anti-anti-communism, antidefense, and so on.

The liberal newspeople, she continued, have many techniques for promoting their causes. For instance, they make great use of "instant analysis": as soon as a speech by a conservative leader has been broadcast, the networks follow it with commentaries by their own analysts refuting the speaker's arguments or minimizing their significance. For another instance, they give plenty of coverage to demonstrations and other happenings staged by antiwar groups, black militants, militant feminists, and the like. Their news specials and documentaries always focus on poverty, racism, pollution, and other things alleged to be wrong with America; they never deal with America's productivity, generosity to foreign countries, success in space exploration, or the many other things that make America look good. And above all, they use the silent treatment: they give only minimal coverage to conservative leaders, organizations, and causes.

Efron, unlike some other conservative media critics, concluded that the strong liberal-Democratic bias of television news is not due to any conspiracy. She had no reason to believe that the leaders of the network news ever meet in secret studios or hotel rooms to plot with leading Democrats and liberals about how to beat the conservatives. The point is, she said, that the people now running the network news have great power. They know it, they enjoy it, and they intend to keep it. So they hire and promote people like themselves and show a solid front against anyone who, like Spiro Agnew or Edith Efron, exposes their slanting of the news. In her words:

> ... The political uniformity of staffing, the almost universal dishonesty that followed the Vice President's Des Moines speech, the rationalized evasions and institutionalized mythologies that serve to cover up the existence of a liberal monopoly in the network news departments, indicate a tacit determination by a ruling intellectual elite to hold onto a position of influence in which it is now entrenched.... There is no conspiracy whatever in network news departments. What we are seeing is: power lust.[9]

A TILT TO THE RIGHT?

Probably less familiar to the general public but equally familiar to academics are another set of critics. They agree with Efron that the network news has a strong political bias, but they believe that it is rigged to defend society's owners and exploiters against all who would hobble or even criticize their machinations. Robert Cirino has made the strongest statement of their indictment,[10] but other charges of bias against liberal and radical leaders and causes have been made by David Altheide, former FCC Commissioner Nicholas Johnson, and by any number of articles and editorials in such "underground" newspapers as the *Village Voice* and the *Berkeley Barb*.

Briefly summarized, Cirino's argument runs as follows: Television broadcasting, like the other "mainstream" mass media in America, is owned and operated by businessmen who have a large stake in maintaining the political and economic status quo against the many "people's movements" that are trying to reform or overthrow it. The media owners make full use of all the weapons at their command to preserve their privileged status, and they are well aware that the television broadcasting they control is one of the most powerful weapons they have.

The researchers, writers, editors, producers, correspondents, and anchormen who produce the network news work for the people who own and run ABC, CBS, and NBC. Every penny the newspeople receive in their salaries and use in their operating budgets is allocated to them by their bosses, and budgets can be cut and newscasters can be fired any time the bosses think that they are getting out of line. Naturally, then, they do as they are told.

"Entertainment" television also plays a major role in keeping ordinary people so besotted with "sit-coms," cop shows, and sports, sports, sports that they have neither the inclination nor the energy to question the Establishment's domination and exploitation. Truly, television has replaced religion as the "opiate of the masses."

The network news also has a part to play in keeping the lid on. On the one hand, it must tell the viewers enough about the events of the day to give them the feeling that they know all they need and want to know about what is going on in the world. But on the other hand, it must not tell them things that will cause them to question the justice of the status quo or do anything to shake it. As Cirino puts it:

> Objectivity and fairness are impossible. Declarations of objectivity and fairness serve only as public relations devices intended to hide from Americans the great advantage of controlling the decisions and tools which create bias. . . . Those who use the techniques of implanting bias in the news cannot be condemned. Rather, it is the communication system that is at fault, allowing the power to create biased news to be monopolized by those who advocate similar viewpoints and priorities. This places the overall bias decidedly to the right of the political spectrum. So those excluded—individuals of solid liberal and radical left viewpoints—are prevented from participating on an equal basis in a competition among ideas. . .[11]

Cirino devotes much of his book to detailing what the network news services do to carry out their masters' orders. They use such devices as taking stories only from the establishment wire services, such as the Associated Press or United Press International; filling much of their short broadcasts with a lot of nonpolitical "human interest" trivia; selecting footage and editing commentaries so as to show the establishment forces as sensible patriots and dissenters as wild and unkempt traitors; and so on.[12]

All these devices promote the Establishment's causes, Cirino says, but its most effective technique is silence. If most of what most people know about politics comes from television, and it does, then the most effective way to suppress antiestablishment ideas and movements is to ignore them. In his words:

> Techniques of persuasion are successful when those who oppose establishment policies do not have access to the media. Such techniques can be offset only when opposing views have an equal opportunity for media use. Could America have ignored racism if the blacks had had at their disposal communication technology and techniques equal to those of the Establishment? Did the white newspaper, newsmagazine, radio, or television audience receive

the black man's viewpoint in an arena where all ideas had an equal chance to be presented?

The Establishment has prevented real public participation by not allowing all ideas to compete fairly for public acceptance. They have allowed free speech, but rendered it worthless by not allowing anti-establishment voices to have *equal* access to the technology of persuasion. The right to speak is of little value if no one is listening.[13]

Structural Bias

As I read the charges of political bias, such as those leveled by Edith Efron from the Right and Robert Cirino from the Left, it seems to me, somewhat to my surprise, that neither side is talking total nonsense. A number of the illustrations they use strike me as reasonably accurate depictions of what I see frequently on the networks' newscasts. Yet the implied picture of a cabal of Agnew's "radic-Libs" or Cirino's "Establishment lackeys" meeting in some smoke-filled studio deciding how best to advance or defeat liberal or conservative causes seems to me ludicrously overdrawn.

In my view, the key to reconciling these discrepant impressions is provided by Paul Weaver's review article of Edith Efron's book. There is no point, he says, in disputing whether her sentence selections and classifications exaggerate the extent of the networks' negative coverage of Nixon's 1968 campaign. Anyone who carefully examines what the networks said has to agree that they said considerably more against Nixon than for him. But what is wrong is Efron's conclusion that the networks did what they did because they wanted to defeat Nixon and elect Humphrey. Weaver puts the point this way:

> ... what Miss Efron's numbers measure is not bias against Nixon himself because of his personality, party, or opinions, *but rather*

Bias in Television News

bias against someone like Nixon for reasons of his journalistically defined situation and identity; and the cause of this bias is not the personal political sentiments of reporters—not their will to unfairness—but rather the nature of the television news form itself. In other words, what Nixon encountered in 1968 was not an essentially political bias: it was essentially *journalistic* bias.[14]

Several other commentators, including me, agree with Weaver that the bias in television news is not so much political as structural. It arises not so much from the newscasters' desire to promote particular political causes as from some special constraints on newscasting.[15] Let us consider three of the most important.

CONSTRAINTS ON TELEVISION NEWS

Economic. Television news in American is what it is largely because of the constraints under which it operates. The first set of these constraints is economic. There are now 727 commercial broadcasting stations and 269 noncommercial stations; but, on the average, about 95 percent of all the receivers are tuned to the commercial stations. These stations and the three great commercial networks, with which 83 percent of all commercial stations are affiliated, are private businesses. As such, their first objective is to make a profit, not to advance conservatism or elect Republicans or outlaw abortions.

Commercial television networks pursue their objectives in several ways: They persuade (and pay) their affiliated stations to broadcast network programs. They attract viewing audiences that are both large and composed mainly of people whose age and social status make them most likely to buy commercial products. They market access to those audiences by selling to advertisers parcels of time during their programs in which the advertisers can broadcast their commercial messages.

Accordingly, the first and most powerful imperative of television is to build and keep the largest possible audiences of the right age and economic status.[16] Audience surveys have confirmed what most television executives have long believed: to attract and hold viewers for newcasts, it is vital to broadcast about matters that interest them and present those matters in the most vivid and attention-compelling manner possible. And there are several rules of thumb about that: For example, pictures of things happening are more interesting than pictures of people talking—hence the dread of showing "talking heads," which is believed to make viewers switch channels faster than about anything else.

One illustration of how powerful is the belief of television news producers that their newscasts must have "good visuals" of events that will interest their viewers is provided by the way they covered the Vietnam War, at least up to the time of the Tet offensive in 1968. From the mid-1960s on, the networks' coverage featured more and more on-the-spot pictures of American troops in combat, sometimes killing the Vietcong enemy and sometimes being killed by them. Some critics have charged that the networks overemphasized the blood and gore because they wanted to horrify their viewers and make them demand that we get out of the war as soon as possible—in other words, because the networks were trying to achieve a political goal. But Michael Mandelbaum gives a more plausible explanation of their motives:

> ... the operational procedures of television news did shape the way that the war was presented to the public. These arose from the needs of the news organizations themselves, not from the political views of those who worked for them. (Television reporters had more or less the same opinions about Vietnam as the country as a whole.) The producers of the news programs encouraged their Saigon correspondents to shoot film of combat, especially before 1968. Combat scenes tended to be more dramatic, more exciting, and therefore—and this was the primary consideration—more likely to attract viewers than other kinds of coverage. Because there was little interest in showing Vietnamese, the subjects of the

combat footage were invariably Americans, who were usually engaged in unspecified, but seemingly successful, military activity.[17]

Another rule of newscasting is that viewers are more interested in the new, the unusual, and the aberrant than the familiar, normal, and hackneyed. As Philip Geyelin of the *Washington Post* puts it:

> This assessment of what people want is not casually arrived at; men who are in business to make money tend to study the market rather carefully, and never mind whether the result is an adequate picture of society. So we hear a great deal more about the campuses where there is unrest than we do about the large majority of campuses where there is quiet. We hear about the problems that are currently, shall we say, fashionable, and we hear about them in such volume that inevitably the picture is distorted and we lose sight of the norm. Airplanes that crash are more interesting than those that don't; young people on heroin are more interesting than those who aren't; those who go to jail rather than be drafted are more interesting than those who don't. And because people will not read or watch things that don't interest them, we don't hear about the norm until we have become so sated by the abnormal that the norm becomes abnormal and therefore interesting.[18]

Time. Another constraint on television news is time. Entertainment programs, of course, draw audiences considerably larger than those for newscasts, except for those few newscasts that provide live coverage of such "blockbuster" events as a face-to-face debate between two presidential candidates or a congressional hearing on the impeachment of a president. Hence the amount of time available for news is strictly limited: prior to 1963 the regular national nightly newscasts were fifteen minutes minus commercials, and since then they have expanded to thirty minutes minus commercials. The national newscasts are almost everywhere preceded by an hour or ninety minutes of local news, weather, and sports. But the network broadcasters have less than thirty minutes in which to cover the major national and international news. The inevitable consequence is that only a little time can be given to any one story: anything over two minutes is most unusual, many stories are given only ten to thirty seconds, and the average is about one minute.

These severe time limits have two powerful effects, both noted in the previous chapter. The first is that the stories can only give what Walter Cronkite called a "headline service": that is, at most they can provide the equivalent of what a typical newspaper story gives in its headline and first and perhaps second paragraph. This was dramatically illustrated when, a few years ago, Richard Salant, the president of CBS News, had the entire script of one evening news broadcast set in newspaper type. He found that it took up less than two columns of the first page of the *New York Times*.[19]

At the present writing all three major networks are considering expanding their nightly newscasts to a full hour minus commercials. If they do so, they will certainly ease their time constraints somewhat, but even so the newsholes for network television news will continue to be much smaller than those for newspapers.

The second effect of television's time constraints is even more important: if the typical newscasts consisted entirely of ten-second snippets, each whipped on and off the tube by itself without being related to anything else on the broadcast or any previous broadcast, the program would be well-nigh unwatchable, rather like having a box of alphabet cereal poured over one's head. Accordingly, as we have seen, each snippet is best presented, whenever possible, as part of a larger ongoing story, as illustrative of a general theme already familiar to the viewer. Thus the stories that are broadcast today make much more sense if they are related to stories that were broadcast yesterday; and, if possible, stories broadcast today should be presented in ways that will readily relate to whatever stories will be broadcast tomorrow.

Bias in Television News

There is no end of such continuity themes. In 1968 it was Nixon the frontrunner against Humphrey the gallant underdog trying to come from behind; in the early 1980s it is the Reagan revolution, the war between the president and Congress, the agonies of the economy, the war between the Arabs and the Israelis, the struggle with the Soviet Union, the strange antics of politicians and young people, and so on. But whatever the continuing story themes may be, all the snippets on each nightly newscast must, if at all possible, be related to them.

Consequently, as we observed in the preceding chapter, where the process of selecting, editing, and interpreting is one part of newspaper news, it is the very essence of television news—not because television producers are eager to sell their political views but because their one-minute stories must make sense if they are to keep their audiences; and they must keep their audiences to survive.

Legal. Some commentators argue that if commercial television stations and networks were constrained only by economic need and limited time there might well be no national newscasts at all. There would be *local* newscasts, for most people are interested in the local weather, local personalities, and the fortunes of the local sports teams. The local news shows, indeed, are quite profitable, and they are about the only shows that most local stations produce for themselves. On the other hand, national and international news is considerably more remote from most people's knowledge and concerns, and yet the national newscasts, in the phenomenon known in the trade as "audience flow," retain most of the audiences from the local newscasts preceding them. As a result, they attract enough advertising to be moderately profitable, though not as profitable as local newscasts.

The fact is, however, that the local stations are compelled by regulations of the Federal Communications Commission (FCC) to broadcast a certain amount of national news, and carrying their network's nightly newscasts is the easiest way to comply. Remember that a television station receives its legal authority to broadcast in the form of a license from the FCC, and that license must be renewed every three years. Among the requirements imposed by the FCC for license renewal is that each station must serve the "public interest, convenience, and necessity" by devoting a certain amount of its time on the air to "public service broadcasting." Precisely what that means is never spelled out in detail, but conversations among the FCC's lawyers and the stations' and networks' lawyers suggest that the FCC will be satisfied with about 5 percent of evening broadcasting time for local news, another 5 percent for national news, and another 10 percent for other nonentertainment programs.[20]

In broadcasting about politics, the stations and networks are constrained by two additional rules. One is the well-known "equal opportunities rule" (sometimes misleadingly called the "equal time rule"), which stipulates that if any time is sold or given to any candidate for an elective office, an equal amount of time must be made available under the same conditions to all other candidates for that office. The only exception to this rule is that broadcasters are allowed to cover, as bona fide news events, press conferences, debates, and similar events not staged or controlled by the broadcasters.

The second rule is the "fairness doctrine," which has a much greater impact on how television news covers politics.[21] The fairness doctrine has two parts: First, broadcasters have an obligation to devote "a reasonable percentage of their broadcast time [see above] to the presentation of news and programs devoted to the consideration and discussion of public issues of interest in the community served by a particular station." Moreover, the FCC declares, "It is this right of the public to be informed rather than any right on the part of the government, any broadcast licensee or any individual member of the public to broadcast his own particular views on any matter, which

Bias in Television News

is the foundation stone of the American system of broadcasting."
The second part of the fairness doctrine declares that in the "presentation of news and comment the public interest require[s] that the licensee must operate on a basis of overall fairness, making his facilities available for the expression of the contrasting views of all responsible elements in the community on the various issues which arise."[22] The precise legal meaning and application of these rules is too complex to explore in detail here. For our purposes the point to note is that most broadcasters have decided that the easiest and surest way to comply with the fairness doctrine is by a practice familiar to all of us and well described by Edward Jay Epstein:

> In the news-room discussions and critiques, political issues are almost always defined by producers as a series of discussions between opposing sides. The expectation is that an issue will be presented in a point-counterpoint format. Any political report lacking this format is usually questioned by producers or news editors, who carefully review outlines and preliminary scripts before the story is completed. The notion that a matter of wide public concern might have only a single defensible side is simply not acceptable.
> ... For example, even when the United States Surgeon-General produced medical evidence indicating that cigarette smoking has damaging effects on health, correspondents had to seek opposing views from the American Tobacco Institute.
> The dialogue, moreover, is limited to two sides. Whenever during my field study correspondents sought to present more than two positions, producers vetoed the idea on the ground that it would be "confusing," and insisted on the formula of two contrasting viewpoints.[23]

This practice, of course, both assumes and promotes the notion that every political issue has two sides and *only* two sides—a proposition that would be supported by few politicians or political philosophers. But as far as the networks and FCC are concerned, when the "pro" and the "anti" side of any issue have been presented, the fairness doctrine has been sat-

49

isfied. As correspondent Bill Plante of CBS News said, "If you have somebody who's calling the president an idiot, you then almost have to have somebody who's saying, 'Well, no he's not; he's really a great statesman.'"[24]

TELEVISION NEWSPEOPLE: BACKGROUNDS AND BELIEFS

Edith Efron, as we have seen, argues that television news has a leftward bias because its personnel are Left-liberals and use the medium to advance the causes they believe in. Robert Cirino argues that television news has a rightward bias because its personnel are the hired hands of the station and network owners and obey orders to play up stories celebrating the status quo and play down stories about its evils and the forces challenging it. And certainly there is at least this much truth in what both sides say: television news, like any other human activity, is strongly influenced by the kind of people who carry on its day-to-day operations and by their views about the requirements of their jobs and the relation of their jobs to the larger society.

What do we know about the people in national television news? From several studies of their backgrounds, training, and beliefs, we can report the following:[25]

Contrary to the Agnew-Efron view, most network news correspondents come from small towns, mainly from the North Central or Northeast states. Most have gone to a public college or university, and very few have attended an Ivy League institution. Most have majored in speech, drama, English, or journalism, and very few have majored in history, economics, or political science. Before the 1960s, most had begun by working for newspapers or wire services and later moved into radio and television news. Since the 1960s, however, most have broken in with a local radio or television station, worked their way into the station's news division, won favorable notice

Bias in Television News

from the networks' recruiters, and been hired by a network for its national operations.

The overwhelming majority have quite apolitical backgrounds. Almost none have a longstanding relationship with a political cause or organization, and almost none have ever worked for a political party or a candidate. Indeed, over two-thirds claim never to have registered to vote as a member of a political party. Most network news recruiters insist that their correspondents should not be strongly committed to any kind of political cause or organization, and the network heads forbid their newspeople to take sides in any political dispute in any way that might reflect on the networks' impartiality.[26] The policy makes good business sense. One of the network newscasts' greatest assets in their competition with each other and with the print press is the public's belief that television news is more trustworthy than any other source of news (see chapter 1). That belief may be all wrong, as the critics from both Left and Right charge, but the networks do all that they can to preserve it as one of their greatest assets.

But what about the personal ideologies of network newspeople? Robert Lichter and Stanley Rothman recently interviewed 240 journalists and broadcasters working for the most influential news media, including the three networks' news departments. Unfortunately for our purposes, their report does not separate the broadcasters' responses from those of the other medias' leaders, but their findings appear, at first glance, to support the Agnew-Efron view. For example, in the four presidential elections from 1964 to 1976, an average of 86 percent of the media leaders voted for the Democratic candidate. On some issues they strongly preferred the liberal sides: large majorities favored affirmative action for blacks, women's rights to have abortions, and vigorous government action to protect the environment. Yet on other issues they were not so liberal: large majorities rejected such tenets of socialism as government ownership of large corporations, equal pay to all workers regardless of their abilities, and the proposition that free enterprise is unfair to workers. They divided evenly on such questions as whether government should guarantee jobs, whether the United States exploits the Third World, and whether the CIA should sometimes undermine hostile foreign governments. But, in what is probably the clincher for some adherents of the Agnew-Efron view, 54 percent described themselves as "liberals" (or "left of center") while only 19 percent called themselves "conservatives."[27]

Yet, before we conclude that this proves the case for liberal political bias in television news, we must ask just how deep and all-controlling is the ideological commitment suggested when newscasters call themselves "liberals." For example, in a frequently quoted interview with *Variety*, Walter Cronkite said that he was a liberal, but he went on to define a "liberal" as "one who is not bound by doctrine or committed to a point of view in advance."[28] Most television newspeople evidently hold a similar view. On the basis of his interviews with people working on the *CBS Evening News* and the *NBC Nightly News*, Herbert Gans reports:

> Journalists generally describe themselves as liberals, but liberalism is a synonym for being independent, open-minded, or both. "I am a classic liberal in the ability to see both sides," one anchorman pointed out. "I don't have a party affiliation, but I am not sure I would even if I were not in the news business."[29]

I agree with the commentators who suggest that if television newspeople have any prevailing political outlook, it is not the liberalism of Edward Kennedy or the Americans for Democratic Action but rather a revised and updated version of the "progressive" outlook that dominated American politics from the 1890s to the 1920s.

Richard Hofstadter's admirable history of the progressive movement emphasizes a number of traits and attitudes that

Bias in Television News

survive in many television newspeople today. For example, the movement was fueled by a generation of popular and influential muckraking journalists, such as Lincoln Steffens and Ida Tarbell, who maintained that the journalist's first obligation is to expose the wrongdoing and mendacity of machine politicians, big businessmen, and other miscreants in high places. Progressive journalists and political activists believed that the decent core of America consists of the ordinary good citizens who genuinely seek what is good for the general welfare. The great enemies of society are the big political machines, the business "trusts," and the other special interests that try to advance their selfish goals at the public's expense by buying elections and corrupting public officials.

The way to save America, the progressives proclaimed, is to reform our political system: First, let the muckraking press dig up and publish all the sordid facts about the greed and lawlessness of the special interests so that honest citizens will know the full extent of the evil they do. Second, let the citizens work together in reform movements to defeat the party machines and fill the public offices with leaders zealous for reform. Third, let the newly-purified governments adopt institutions—notably, the initiative, referendum, and direct primary—that will enable the people to rule directly whenever the parties and the government are unresponsive to their wishes. Finally, when the system is thus reformed and purified, it will no longer be the tool of the special interests but will become what it was meant to be: the people's instrument for promoting the general welfare.[30]

Like Herbert Gans and others, I detect similar attitudes underlying the way many television newspeople in the 1980s view their professional roles and deal with politics. As Gans puts it:

> That modern journalists should invoke values from the turn of the century does not suggest that the profession is operating with old-

fashioned ideas, for Progressivism is hardly dead.... Today these values also serve journalism as a profession, giving it a respected social role. Insofar as journalists are defenders of a set of values, they are more than technicians who transmit information from sources to audiences. Contemporary journalists do not, for the most part, see themselves as reformers; but the ones I studied were proud whenever a story resulted in official investigations and in legislative or administrative reform. Then, too, Progressivism was, among other things, a professional movement that aimed to bring experts into politics and government, and its values enhance the professionalism of journalism.... Also, Progressive ideology sidesteps or cuts across the partisanship of the political parties; it was, and continues to be, attractive to people who, like journalists, regard themselves as political independents.[31]

In the end, however, what matters is not what television newspeople *believe* but what they *do* in portraying politics on the air. Michael Jay Robinson correctly reminds us that "press *behavior*—not opinion—is the key. Bias that counts must be in the copy, not just in the minds of those who write it." And his study of bias in television's coverage of the 1980 presidential election came to about the same conclusion as Hofstetter's study of bias in coverage of the 1972 election: the networks' reports showed no continuing or consistent political bias for any of the major candidates or parties, but rather a kind of general bias against all the major candidates and a near-complete silence about the minor party candidates, including such super-liberals as Benjamin Spock in 1972 and Barry Commoner in 1980. As Robinson summed it up, "[the networks' news reports] were cynical, yes; but liberal, no . . . over the long haul the national press is biased against everybody, but in near equal proportions."[32]

For all of these reasons, then, it seems to me that network television news does have a bias, but it is not a political bias in favor of liberalism or conservatism. It is instead a structural bias, arising from the way television is organized in the United States, from the economic, organizational, and legal circum-

Bias in Television News

stances in which it operates, and from the kind of people who are attracted to its special opportunities and satisfy its special requirements. And that bias tends to produce a special kind of picture of what politics is all about.

POLITICS ACCORDING TO TELEVISION NEWS

Paul Weaver has written the best brief characterization I have seen on what television news thinks is the essential nature of American politics. In his words:

> [According to television news] politics is essentially a game played by individual politicians for personal advancement, gain, or power. The game is a competitive one, and the players' principal activities are those of calculating and pursuing strategies designed to defeat competitors and to achieve their goals (usually election to public office). Of course, the game takes place against a backdrop of governmental institutions, public problems, policy debates, and the like, but these are noteworthy only insofar as they affect, or are used by, players in pursuit of the game's rewards. The game is played before an audience—the electorate—which controls most of the prizes, and players therefore constantly attempt to make a favorable impression. In consequence, there is an endemic tendency for players to exaggerate their good qualities and to minimize their bad ones, to be deceitful, to engage in hypocrisies, to manipulate appearances; though inevitable, these tendencies are bad tendencies . . . and should be exposed. They reduce the electorate's ability to make its own discriminating choices, and they may hide players' infractions of the game's rules, such as those against corruption and lying.[33]

Let us look a bit more closely at each main feature of Weaver's depiction of television's political map.

The Main Players Are Individuals. Individual persons are ideal subjects for television. They are easily interviewed, taped, and dramatized. Moreover, the audience feels it understands them; after all, the viewers are themselves individuals, know other individuals, and feel that they understand people.

On the other hand, a group or an organization is an abstraction, for it consists of only certain common qualities abstracted from the different bundles of qualities possessed by the various persons who compose it. Consequently, television must present any group or organization either in words alone or in pictures of some kind of crowd. The newscasts usually personify an organization through interviews with its leaders and perhaps also with some of its dissident members. In this way, the pictorial requirements of the medium and its economic need to hold the audience require television news to present politics as a contest in which the main players are individuals, not groups or organizations.

Thus, television presents a political party's national nominating convention not as another of a long series of occasions in which the party has met and chosen its standard bearers, but as this year's contest among candidates, faction leaders, and special interest leaders, with little reference to the past or future. A presidential campaign is presented as a contest between two candidates, not two political parties. By far the most exciting events of any such campaign are the "great debates" in which the two leading men stand side by side on the same television set so that the viewers can compare directly how they look and sound as well as hear what they have to say. No television producer would dream of covering, unless he had to, a series of national debates in which a number of leaders of both parties, not just the presidential candidates, would discuss the issues raised by the parties' platforms. Every viewer knows that the platforms are complicated and boring and have little to do with what the election is all about, which is who is going to win. The story is Reagan and Carter, not the Republican party and Democratic party.

Self-Interest Is the Spur. Why the political players do what they do, their basic motives and objectives, is no mystery to television newspeople. Edward Jay Epstein reports from his interviews with NBC's correspondents and producers:

Bias in Television News

Almost any governmental act was generally ultimately attributed by correspondents in interviews to a single motive: winning elections. In this view, politics is seen as a "game plan" for defeating determined opponents, rather than as a process for distributing values or resolving conflicts between interested parties. Economic programs, government reorganizations, Supreme Court appointments and foreign policy are commonly explained in terms of an officeholder attempting to attract potential voters to his side. Neither ideology nor personal commitment to substantive goals were considered to be realistic explanations of such acts.[34]

So the interesting question for television news is never what the politicians are after; they are always after power, material gain, and, above all, the votes they need to get what they want. The interesting subject matter is the notions of strategy and tactics that lead the politicians to do what they are doing. And the most interesting questions are: who is ahead, who is falling back, who is gaining, who is going to win?

"Horse Race" Journalism. Some commentators have said that the best way to understand why television reports politics, especially election campaigns, as it does is to recognize that it is a form of sports reporting. Or, as some have put it, the networks have long since abandoned all other approaches to political reporting in favor of "horse race" journalism—that is, concentrating mainly on who is winning and why and paying little attention to what difference it makes.[35] There is a good deal of evidence to support this. For example, Thomas Patterson's study of the medias' treatment of the 1976 presidential election shows that television news gave twice as much coverage to stories about strategy, logistics, and who was winning than to stories about where the candidates stood on the issues or about their previous records in public office.[36]

To take just one example, many people have complained that the networks in 1976 and 1980 paid much more attention to the Iowa caucuses in January and the New Hampshire primary in February than to the nine state primaries held in June, despite the fact that the June primaries chose over one-fifth of all the delegates and Iowa and New Hampshire together chose less than 3 percent.[37] Why? Patterson explains:

> ... the press has a bias toward hard events. Until New Hampshires happens and the first votes are taken, the press must rely on soft indicators, such as the candidates' poll stands and finances, that have only a potential relationship to the candidates' success. Given its traditional emphasis on activity, the press would prefer to focus on actual outcomes, even if they involve a few voters, narrow margins, and a questionable relationship to the thinking of the national electorate. "The early caucuses and primaries are seen as the first 'hard news' stories of the presidential race, a perception which almost guarantees an inflated value placed on the results of these events," writes Christopher Arterton. "The unrepresentative nature of the early contests is neglected because *finally* the contest has begun."[38]

TELEVISION'S ANTIPOLITICIAN AND ANTIESTABLISHMENT BIASES

Finally, does seeing American politics and politicians in this light involve any substantive bias that might materially affect Americans' political "cognitive maps" and, through them, the American way of politics? I believe that there are at least two such biases. The first clear bias, I believe, is not against liberals or conservatives or Democrats or Republicans, but against *all* politicians, and especially against those most identified with electoral politics. After many hours of interviewing television correspondents, Edward Jay Epstein summed up their view thus:

> The working hypothesis almost universally shared among correspondents is that politicians are suspect; their public images probably false, their public statements disingenuous, their moral pronouncements hypocritical, their motives self-serving, and their promises ephemeral. Correspondents thus see their jobs to be to expose politicians by unmasking their disguises, debunking their claims and piercing their rhetoric. In short, until proven otherwise,

political figures of any party or persuasion are presumed to be deceptive opponents. This generalized cynicism toward politicians—who are often called "frauds," "phonies," and "liars" in the newsroom—may account for a substantial share of the on-the-air derogation, rather than any partisan politics of the correspondents.[39]

Epstein adds a significant point. When a politician is interviewed by a newspaper reporter, he knows that he and his views will reach the public only through the reporter's story. If he convinces the reporter that he is an honest man with a case deserving respect and attention, that is how the story will come out. But it the reporter thinks he is stupid or hypocritical, it will come out quite differently. The politician thus has a major stake in trying to make the best possible impression on the newspaper reporter. An interview on television is different. The politician knows that at least something of what he says and how he looks will be broadcast directly to the viewers, so he can address them directly without giving all of his attention to the impression he is making on the correspondent. Correspondents are well aware of this and most of them resent politicians' untiring efforts to "use" television interviews in this way. Consequently politicians' interviews with network correspondents are more likely to assume an adversary character than are their interviews with print journalists.[40]

I know of no systematic study of the matter, but I believe that entertainment television also has a distinct antipolitician bias. Most of the live politicians that appear in situation comedies and dramas are portrayed as pompous, windy, hypocritical, and self-seeking buffoons. Dead politicians, like Abraham Lincoln, John F. Kennedy, and even Harry Truman, are portrayed much more sympathetically. Truman once succinctly defined a "statesman" as "a dead politician" and while that may not be adequate for a political science textbook, it does quite well for television dramas.

Then too, in how many television dramas is the hero a person who stands firm for a principle, courageously resisting the efforts of other people to persuade him to conceal the truth or back off from justice in the name of compromise and expedience? I can recall a great many such dramas, and so, I imagine, can everyone else. On the other hand, in how many dramas is the hero a person who juggles many conflicting values and manages to find a compromise that all can live with? I can think of only one: the episode in "Upstairs, Downstairs" in which the Bellamy family visits the castle of a Scottish laird whose staff treats them badly, hoping they will leave before they can discover that the staff are poaching salmon from their master's private stream. Hudson, the Bellamy's butler, discovers the poaching and cuts a deal with the laird's staff: he will keep quiet about their lawbreaking, and they will take good care of the Bellamys. This may not be the only example of political compromise ever celebrated in a television drama, but it is the only one I can recall. And even it, let us remember, was produced by a British company.

In any event, it is clear that both real life and fictional politicians are rarely presented favorably on American television. The impact this may have on ordinary Americans' attitudes toward politics and the people who make it work is something we shall consider in chapter 3.

Television newspeople also have an antiestablishment bias: that is, they view with special suspicion whatever political leaders and organizations seem most powerful at the moment. The sources of this bias seem clear. The people who write, produce, and present television news consider themselves to be journalists, doing essentially what print journalists do, but doing it under more difficult circumstances. One of the oldest and most persistent beliefs of journalists (and many other Americans as well) is the conviction that one of the primary professional obligations of any news medium—indeed, a

Bias in Television News

prime reason for its existence in a free society—is to act as the public's watchdog over government. Ordinary people have neither the time, the access, nor the special experience necessary to uncover the reality behind what politicians and bureaucrats say they are doing. If the people do not know what is really going on they cannot know who the rascals are, let alone throw them out. In this sense, true democratic government cannot exist without an informed public opinion; and it is the solemn duty of the press to provide the information that the public must have. Thus, as we have seen, the muckrakers' exposés in the early 1900s provided the foundation for the progressives' reforms. And the investigative journalists' revelations of the 1970s were at least as important for the post-Vietnam and post-Watergate reforms.[41]

Accordingly, all journalists, including network newspeople, feel that their job is, not to make it easier for government to make and carry out its policies, but to probe deeply and tirelessly into what government is really doing so that the people will know. This means that they will not be moved by complaints of public officials that snooping by the news media is making it hard to get the government's work done, for they feel obligated by the highest standards of their profession to assume an adversary posture toward government. They may back off occasionally from some subjects, as when the *New York Times* acceded to President John F. Kennedy's request that the paper not print what it had dug up about the planned invasion of the Bay of Pigs. But most newspeople believe that most of the time their first obligation is to discover and print or broadcast whatever important information they can find about what the government is really doing.[42]

Newspeople generally feel that this is reason enough for their persistent adversary posture toward government and politicians, but television newspeople have additional reasons for their antiestablishment posture. If you are in the business of describing "horse races," upsets by long-shots are a lot more interesting than favorites winning by twenty lengths. Public conflicts between clashing principles are more interesting than secretly-made compromises resolving problems. New names, new faces, and new issues are more interesting than the ones that have been around for years.

One of many illustrations for this point is the high exposure and kid-gloves treatment Jimmy Carter received in the early months of his drive for the 1976 Democratic nomination, compared with the much harsher treatment he encountered once he had the nomination locked up—and ever since. As Thomas Cronin correctly points out, it was not Carter the liberal or Carter the conservative who was the victim of the switch. It was Carter the long-shot who became Carter the frontrunner. As Cronin says:

> Unwittingly or not, the media often levels front-running candidates. In a variation of the adversary relations theme, it is as if the press and television have a greater obligation to probe, scrutinize, and pick apart the latest celebrity. [Pulitzer prizes] don't go to journalists who deflate dark horses, but to those who expose the leaders. Hence the notion of the primaries as a multimedia survival course, perhaps better suited to knocking people off than permitting the best to rise.[43]

Conclusion

In all these respects, the network newspeople take the antiestablishment stance that most journalists take, in part because they feel it is their professional obligation and in part because it makes for more interesting stories, more Emmies, larger audiences, and all the good things that larger audiences bring. In recent years, however, the networks have come to play this

Bias in Television News

adversary role more powerfully for more people than the print media. Michael Robinson puts the point forcefully:

> ... although it has been only recently and partially documented, network journalism tends to be more "anti-establishment" than print journalism, especially compared to the non-prestige newspapers.... One important outcome of this usurpation of the parties by the media has been that network news has emerged as "the loyal opposition," more so even than the party out of office. *It is now the networks that act as the shadow cabinet.*[44]

Surely the bias of a loyal opposition is a bias by any definition, and one that is far more structural than ideological. And just as surely is it understandable, predictable, and constant.

The late senator from Ohio, Robert Alphonso Taft, did not leave many quotable maxims, but he did leave one that should help us know what to expect from television news in the future. "The business of the opposition," he said, "is to oppose."[45]

In the American way of politics in the 1980s, that's the way it is.

Chapter 3

Television's Impact on American Political Culture

IF, as I have argued in the preceding chapters, political reality for most Americans consists of what television tells them about politics, and if television usually presents politics from a special perspective about the essential nature of the political game, then we would surely expect the American way of politics to be significantly different since the advent of television in the 1950s from the way it was before World War II. The task of this and the next two chapters is to detail some of the major impacts television has had on American political behavior and institutions.

We begin with television's impact on our political culture. Political scientists use that term to denote the basic attitudes of our people toward politics, including their beliefs about the way the political world really works and their preferences for

Television's Impact on American Political Culture

some political institutions and policies over others.[1] Since these prevailing beliefs and preferences constitute perhaps the most powerful single determinant of Americans' political behavior, it is the first place we should look for signs of television's political impact.

The Information Avalanche

Some critics of television, as we noted in chapter 2, attack television's coverage of politics as excessively biased in favor of particular ideologies, policies, parties, and candidates. Others attack it as too sensational, too focused on personalities instead of issues, and too superficial to be worthy of a serious person's attention. Some complain that television does not give us enough coverage to satisfy the great hunger for political information that many of us have. Yet it is possible that television news puts out considerably more political information than most Americans really want, but they find hard to avoid; and being told more than they want to know about politics may have a significant effect on their interest and desire to participate in it.

Let us consider this possibility in the light of some facts.

ORIGINS AND GROWTH OF TELEVISION NEWS

As Richard Rubin reminds us, television journalism, unlike print journalism, developed out of the entertainment business, not the newsgathering business. Even today the comment most likely to arouse the irate denials of television newspeople is being told that they are in "show business" rather than "journalism." From television's first acceleration in the late 1940s until the early 1960s, the national networks broadcast only the minimum amount of public affairs programming, including news, necessary to satisfy the FCC. Until 1963 each network broadcast only one regular news show per day, and each was only fifteen minutes long. The newscasts mostly featured reporters reading news reports taken mainly from the wire services and occasionally from leading newspapers, and few films and even fewer graphics were used to make them visually interesting. They were essentially radio newscasts read in front of cameras.

The news divisions' budgets were small, and the network chiefs regarded the newscasts as legally necessary and perhaps even prestigious—there was, after all, the "See It Now" series of Edward R. Murrow on CBS. But they lost money, and a prudent business could spend only so much on prestige.

In the early 1960s, however, things began to change. The networks' live coverage of political events, such as the parties' national nominating conventions and the Kennedy-Nixon debates of 1960, brought them not only critical applause but also respectably large audiences and, consequently, respectable revenues from the advertising time they sold during these broadcasts. The news divisions ultimately persuaded the networks' executives that if the nightly newscasts were given bigger budgets, better production facilities, and more time they might eventually even make money. So in 1963 all three networks expanded their nightly newscasts from fifteen to thirty minutes and began to seek ways of making them more attractive visually and in other ways. The consequent increase in the sheer amount of their coverage in politics has continued and expanded ever since.[2]

Indeed, in 1981–1982, CBS News decided that it would be a good idea to expand their nightly newscasts from thirty minutes to a full hour (minus commercials, of course), and if they had done so it is likely that NBC and ABC would have followed suit. However, a large majority of CBS's local affiliated stations were unwilling to give up the profitable evening time (from 7:30 to 8:00 P.M. in most areas) that the expanded na-

Television's Impact on American Political Culture

tional newscasts would take, and so the idea was shelved for the time being. Even so, by the early 1980s a good deal of television time was given to local and national newscasts.

LOCAL NEWS AND NATIONAL NEWS TODAY

A majority of the total broadcasting time devoted to news today is taken up by programs produced by local stations, including network affiliates, not by the networks' news divisions. For example, a typical local network affiliate's newscasts in a typical broadcasting weekday occupy the following time slots:

6:00 A.M. to 7:00 A.M. (Eastern time): local news
7:00 A.M. to 9:00 A.M.: a network entertainment/news show (such as NBC's "Today" and ABC's "Good Morning, America", with four five-minute national news slots, two five-minute local news slots, and two or three five-minute interviews of public figures on current national political issues.[3]
12:00 noon to 12:30 P.M.: local news
5:00 or 5:30 P.M. to 7:00 P.M.: local news
7:00 P.M. to 7:30 P.M.: national network news
11:00 P.M. to 11:30 P.M.: local news
1:30 A.M.: national network news

This adds up to about 100 minutes (minus commercials) of national network news a day,[4] compared with from 165 to 240 minutes of local news. There are good business reasons for this distribution. Edward Jay Epstein's research in the 1960s found that the local news shows were among the few (in many cases the only) shows of any kind produced by the local stations. They still are. Moreover, local newscasts were and are produced quite lavishly, typically with a number of camera crews and mobile units in action every day, expensive sets, a sizeable stable of reporters, and a well-paid varsity team of anchors, weather forecasters, and sports commentators.

In the 1980s, to be sure, the national newscasts have become modestly profitable, although not so profitable as the local newscasts. But what Epstein reported for the late 1960s remains largely true for the 1980s: local newscasts have large and loyal audiences, and their importance as "lead-ins" to the network newscasts is shown by the fact that the popularity of a particular affiliate's local newscast has more to do with the size of the audience for its network's national newscasts than any of the latter's special merits or deficiencies.[5]

Local newscasts differ from networks' newscasts in several respects. They are less political, in that the local newscasts pay much less attention than the national newscasts to politics and much more attention to sports, "human interest" stories, how-to-do-it features, and the like. The local newscasts, at least until recently, have generally been more concerned with getting and keeping the largest possible audiences than with sober and professional presentation and analysis of the news. The "happy news" approach, featuring a good deal of on-camera chit-chat and badinage among the performers, has been widely adopted as the most effective means to that end, and one sometimes hears national network broadcasters deplore the locals' overly jocund and superficial coverage. Evidently the local audiences like it, for local newscasters show little disposition to change their ways.

It is not surprising, then, that the national newscasts have a much higher proportion of political stories than do the local newscasts. Perhaps more surprising is the fact that the national newscasts have a substantially higher proportion of political news than do the front pages of leading national newspapers. Richard Rubin compared the leading stories on the "CBS Evening News" with the three leading front-page newspapers stories in leading papers between 1963 and 1975 and found that, by margins of two and three to one, the CBS newscasts had higher proportions of political stories—that is, "stories that are linked to either national political figures or institutions, e.g., the activities of congressional committees, actions taken by the president, or other partisan activities going on in Washington"—than the newspapers' front pages.[6]

Television's Impact on American Political Culture

Other factors contribute to the national networks' tendency to broadcast a great deal of political information. One is well illustrated by a scene we shall never see on our television screens: ten minutes into the "CBS Evening News with Dan Rather" the handsome anchorman smiles disarmingly at the camera and says, "Ladies and Gentlemen, nothing else of great importance has happened in the world today, so we are shortening our newscast by twenty minutes. During the rest of our time you will see a documentary film on the plight of teaching assistants in American universities, and we hope to be back tomorrow night with our normal thirty minutes of news."

The scene will not take place because, come what may, CBS News must and will fill its thirty-minute newshole every night, regardless of how many newsworthy stories may be available for any particular night's show. Newspapers can, to some degree, expand or contract their column-inches of news to fit the stories available, but an iron law of television is that the newsholes must be filled with something. In the great tradition of the parent enterprise, the show must go on. So if there are only one or two—or no—major political stories, the show's production team can be counted on to fill up the available time with the most important (least unimportant?) stories it can find. And since their jobs, as well as their professional reputations, are at stake, who can blame them?

TELLING US MORE THAN WE WANT TO KNOW

What is the impact of the abundant flow of political information regularly turned out by national newscasts and, to a lesser degree, by local newscasts? Perhaps we can begin our answer to that question by recognizing that most of the major studies of the attitudes and behavior of mass publics find that a substantial majority of Americans are, most of the time, not very interested in politics. They typically believe that, except in times of great crisis, what presidents and congressmen do or fail to do affects little or not at all the significant aspects of their personal lives—going to school, getting a job, getting married, setting up a home, raising children, staying healthy, watching television, and so on. They personally deal with government on only a few occasions, usually unpleasant, as when they pay a parking ticket or fill out Form 1040. It is not that they are *totally* uninterested in politics; after all, well over half of them (an estimated 120 million) voluntarily watched the televised Reagan-Carter debate in the 1980 presidential campaign, and in a 1982 poll 36 percent of the respondents said that they "follow what's going on in government most of the time," while another 36 percent said they follow it "some of the time."[7] It is rather that they tend to see politics as a moderately interesting spectator sport rather than as a life-and-death struggle over matters of basic personal concern.[8]

This is always a difficult point to make to the kind of people who are likely to read a book like this. There is no doubt that to a minority of Americans, politics is a serious contest over matters of great importance, not only for Americans but for people all over the world who are touched by American culture and power. But more than that, some of us find politics—its conflicts, its personalities, its causes and consequences—fascinating to watch quite apart from how it affects us personally. So we watch several newscasts every day; we regularly read the political stories, editorials, and op-ed commentaries in one or more newspapers; we may even subscribe to a political magazine, such as the *Nation* or the *National Review*; we enroll in political science or political sociology courses; we talk politics every chance we get; we may even read books like this one. And we sometimes find it hard to remember—and even harder not to deplore—the fact that most Americans are much less interested in politics than we.

Edwin Diamond, a distinguished scholar of mass communications and society, learned this point well from one of his

Television's Impact on American Political Culture

students. After he had lectured on the low salience of politics for most Americans, the student wrote to him:

> One point you brought out and is a fairly common point is the seeming apathy of the public in general toward the day-to-day affairs of government. Having grown up in a small town in Michigan, let me suggest one possible reason for this on the part of some of the citizens and to do so let me make an analogy. Many people buy automobiles *only* as a means of transportation and have no interest in how it works, if the color is red or blue, etc., and the only time those people become at all involved in how the garage services the car is when it does not fulfill the basic transportation need.
>
> The point is that some people may well view our government as a function to take care of certain needs and really do not want to be involved with the day-to-day carrying out of this function any more than the servicing of [their] cars. And although that is often viewed with alarm by those who for various reasons have an interest in the day-to-day workings of the government, the other fellow may well feel he pays good taxes so that certain functions can be taken care of and he wants no personal hobby-like intrigue with the government process and really wants to spend some of his free time and $ doing things which appeal to *him personally* and he probably can't understand why anyone would want to get all wrapped up in the governmental process when there is fishing, T.V., little league, etc.[9]

Yet the unpolitical majority watch the same local and national television newscasts we politics buffs watch (though they are much less likely than we to watch an hour-long documentary about politics). So the same political information that is lavished on us is lavished on them. But there is one big difference between us, which was noted in chapter 1: they mainly get their political information, not because they are eager for it and seek it out, but because it is broadcast when they happen to be watching television. Moreover, the political stories are mixed with weather forecasts, sports reports, human interest stories, and the like. The political stories usually last only a minute or two, and since watching television is, a

71

passive, undemanding kind of activity, it is simply too much trouble to tune out the political stuff for that minute or two until something more interesting comes on.

Some analysts argue that not only the sheer volume of political information but the manner in which it is presented has a certain numbing effect—what might be called the "crying-wolf effect"; Doris Graber describes it thus:

> Most people do not need detailed knowledge of current affairs for either their job or their social relationships. They would rather discuss sports, or the weather, or gossip than politics, which they see as a touchy topic. So they scan the news for major crises but do not try to remember specific facts. When people sense that events have a large impact on their lives or when they need information to make voting choices, political interest and learning perk up quickly and often dramatically.

The network newscasters are aware of this, Graber says, and so to attract and hold large audiences they have to give their viewers a lot of facts *and* make them all seem important. Graber continues:

> The presentation of media information also contributes to the difficulty people experience in learning from the media. First of all, there is the sheer bulk of new information. People are deluged, day after day, with important and trivial news, most of which is touted as "important." The constant crisis atmosphere numbs the interest and creates jaded boredom.
>
> The fact that stories are told in disconnected snippets further complicates the task of making sense out of them and integrating them into existing knowledge. This is especially true when stories are complex. People who feel that they cannot understand what is happening are discouraged from spending time reading or listening. Featuring conflicting stories and interpretations without giving guidance to the audience is another deterrent to learning.[10]

We shall return to this point and its consequences later in this chapter.

Television's Impact on American Political Culture

The Fast-Forward Effect

Every video cassette recorder has a "fast-forward" feature that enables viewers to speed up the videotape so that they can rapidly pass by unwanted material and get to the parts they want to see. The feature is not merely convenient, it symbolizes what the medium conveys, in that television coverage itself has the effect of speeding up the worlds it portrays, including the world of politics.

We noted in chapter 2 that television's time constraints force network newspeople to present political news mainly in quick successions of one-minute and two-minute stories. Similarly, the typical entertainment drama poses a problem, works it through, and arrives at a dramatically satisfying solution in one or two hours minus commercials. Even the relatively leisurely and serious political documentaries present the essential facts and the "pro" and "con" sides (the "fairness doctrine" again) of a political or economic issue in an hour or two minus (fewer) commercials.

We cannot say with scientific certainty precisely what effects this way of portraying politics and life has had on American political culture, but it is hard to avoid the impression that Americans' expectations of politics and government have been speeded up considerably since the advent of television. For example, we seem more and more to demand quick and final solutions to complex and intransigent problems; we are more impatient with partial solutions or solutions that are too long in coming; and we are prone to dump leaders who do not produce soon enough the results they promised when they were seeking our votes.

David Littlejohn concludes that this "fast-forward" effect of television has a profound impact on people's tolerance for the many untidy aspects of real life, including politics:

I believe (I do not know) that [television reduces] one's tolerance to stillness and silence, to mental space and irresolution. By increasing one's tolerance to noise, chopped variety, imagistic chaos, and the atomization of time, they may shrivel up patience and tolerance generally—tolerance of a thousand and one "real world" situations: overlong meetings, amateur entertainment, unfamous people, ineloquent politicians, unsmooth conversation, scoreless ties in sports—without instituting in the viewer the least urge or impulse to correct an uncomfortable situation. He can always stay home and change the channel.[11]

In chapter 5 we shall consider the consequences of the "fast-forward" effect upon such matters as how much time presidents and other politicians have to put their programs in place and produce results good enough to convince people that they are on the right track, and upon how long they can reasonably hope to stay in office.

The Way We See Politicians

Most Americans have never had a high opinion of politicians as a class, although they have sometimes admired a particular politician enough to call him or her a "statesman" or "leader."[12] The evidence crops up in all sorts of places. For example, *Webster's Dictionary*, after giving first a neutral definition of a politician as "a person . . . actively engaged in conducting the business of government," adds a second definition that probably seems right to many more people: "a person primarily interested in political office from selfish or other narrow usu. short-run interests."[13] For another example, in its listing for "politician" *Roget's Thesaurus* gives such unflattering synonyms as "party hack," "wheel-horse," "grafter," "spoils-monger," "power broker," "influence peddler," "wheeler-dealer," "finagler," "wire-puller," and "ward heeler."[14]

Television's Impact on American Political Culture

One recent Gallup poll reported that only 23 percent of the American people would like to see their children go into politics as a life's work, and another reported that the only kinds of people who are thought to have even lower standards of ethics and honesty than politicians are advertisers, car salespeople, and union leaders![15] And Edwin Diamond points out that most Americans believed that the Watergate revelations of the early 1970s not only exposed the particular evildoings of Richard Nixon and some of his supporters but told us something about politicians in general as well:

> After the first three months of the Senate's Watergate hearings, involving 35 witnesses and 7,500 pages of testimony, a Louis Harris poll showed that a large majority of the American public agreed, at that point in time, with the proposition that "dirty campaign tactics exist among Democrats and Republicans and the Nixon campaign people were no worse, except that they got caught at it. . . ." Seven out of ten Americans adopted this remarkably wrong-headed conclusion even though a mountain of information had been publicly accumulated about Republican "dirty tricks" and not one molehill of information had been gathered about illegal Democratic campaign tactics.[16]

A number of political scientists have long tried to counteract this traditional defamation of politicians. In classes, books, and articles, they have tried to point out that, used properly, the term "politician" refers to all persons who are directly engaged in the process of making public policy, that only a small minority of politicians are stupid, venal, or corrupt, and that politicians, more than any group in our society, do the work that makes democratic government possible. Several decades ago Judge Arthur Vanderbilt founded the Citizenship Clearing House, an organization operated mainly by political scientists, which sought to persuade college students that politics is a necessary and honorable profession in which they should participate fully and proudly. But whatever success the CCH may or may not have had with students, it had no visible impact whatever on the poor opinion most Americans have of politicians—or on the way they are portrayed by television journalists.

Most of the people who produce and broadcast television news fully share the traditional American distaste for politicians as a class. Certainly television characteristically portrays politicians as being motivated mainly or solely by their eagerness to win votes, and seldom or never by any desire to promote the public interest.[17]

If most Americans learn most of what they know about politics and politicians from what they see and hear on television, then surely their traditional antipathy toward politicians as a class is confirmed, reinforced, and perhaps even intensified by the way television portrays politicians. There is good direct evidence to support this point: Michael Robinson used data generated by a sample-survey study of the electorate in the 1968 presidential election conducted by the Center for Political Studies of the University of Michigan. He divided the respondents into those who used television as their main or sole source of information about politics and those who used several other sources (such as newspapers, magazine, and conversations with friends) as well. He found a clear and strong inverse relationship:

> Those who rely upon television in following politics are more confused and more cynical than those who do not. And those who rely totally upon television are the most confused and cynical of all. The differences among the groups run generally between 10 percent and 15 percent. When looking at respondents with a similar level of education the differences diminish, but they do not disappear.[18]

Some analysts make a convincing case for the proposition that television's constant denigration of politicians' motives, words, and deeds does more than merely confirm politicians'

Television's Impact on American Political Culture

already-established poor reputation; it also lowers public confidence in the very institutions of government itself. Robinson concludes:

> The themes which the networks offer are predominantly negative. That alone would suggest that our opinions about our government, our society and ourselves would tend not to be positive. But the more important aspect of thematic reporting is inherent conflict, either personal or organizational. My own experiments with viewers suggest that this personal and institutional conflict, so appropriate and essential to thematic reporting, is profoundly disturbing to the audience, especially the Inadvertent Audience. The news organization and the journalist may believe that conflict between Senators or business leaders or bureaucrats is good copy; perhaps it is. But among the inadvertent viewers I suggest that this copy takes on a different and more profound meaning. The general effects are, I surmise, not only sustained viewing but growing political estrangement and a desire to return to a bygone era of political purity and decency, an era which is undoubtedly over-romanticized by the networks and all the mass media.[19]

The political sociologists Kurt and Gladys Lang broaden Robinson's point. They contend that television focuses on clashes between politicians as the very heart of political news. That, in turn, makes politics even more confusing for most viewers. It thereby enhances their feeling that their inability to understand what the squabbling is all about proves that ordinary people are being manipulated by sinister forces. In the Langs' words:

> The way television handles the day-to-day flow of news by presenting a series of headline stories tends to highlight the unusual and extraordinary. Conflicts and crises predominate. Balanced presentation, that hallmark of good television reporting which gives equal time to charges and counter-charges, can, where contextual interpretation is inadequate, create a feeling that political events are beyond the scope of ordinary comprehension. Nor is the full coverage of an event enough to neutralize the inclinations of the

chronically distrustful. It may only abet the tendency of viewers low in political competence to see in what they cannot understand proof that they are being manipulated.

Hence, television's style in chronicling political events can affect the fundamental orientation of the voter toward his government, it can undermine or bolster public confidence in the viability of political institutions, and in the ability of political leaders to discharge their responsibilities.... This kind of distrust, which is of a distinctly projective nature, has its roots in the complexities of political life, complexities that lie beyond the understanding of all but the most politically sophisticated. The media, we contend, can stir up in individuals defensive reactions by their emphasis on crisis and conflict in lieu of clarifying normal decision-making processes.[20]

So it seems. Just about every study of the matter shows that the public's level of confidence and trust in our political institutions has declined sharply since the 1950s. For example, since 1958 the University of Michigan's Center for Political Studies has periodically asked national samples of American adults the question, "How much of the time can you trust the government in Washington? Just about always, most of the time, some of the time, or hardly ever?" Those answering "just about always" or "most of the time" are classified as "trusting," and those answering "hardly ever" are classified as cynical. The results over time are shown in table 3.1.

TABLE 3.1
Trust in Government, 1958–1978

Attitude	1958 (%)	1964 (%)	1968 (%)	1970 (%)	1972 (%)	1974 (%)	1976 (%)	1978 (%)
Cynical	11	19	26	36	36	50	53	52
In-Between	25	18	24	25	24	24	23	26
Trusting	58	61	48	38	38	24	22	19

SOURCE: Warren E. Miller, "Misreading the Public Pulse," *Public Opinion*, Oct./Nov. 1979, p. 11.

Television's Impact on American Political Culture

The data in table 3.1 show a continuous and precipitous drop in public confidence and trust in government since the late 1950s. For another example, since 1966 the Louis Harris poll has been asking people whether, with respect to each of a number of the nation's institutions, "as far as the people in charge of running [each] are concerned, would you say you have a great deal of confidence, only some confidence or hardly any confidence at all." In 1966, 50 percent expressed a great deal of confidence in the U.S. Supreme Court, and 42 percent gave the same answer about Congress. From then on both figures declined steadily, and in 1982 they stood at 25 percent for the Supreme Court and 13 percent for Congress.[21]

We cannot, of course, say that television's portrayal of politics has been the sole or even the main cause of this steep decline in popular confidence and trust in our political and governmental institutions and leaders. After all, there has been a good deal of bad news about both to report in recent years—assassinations, Vietnam, Watergate, Abscam, inflation, high interest rates, high unemployment, our inability to rescue our countrymen held hostage in Iran, and so on. But it is hard not to put two facts side by side: one is the fact that the age of television began in the 1950s and reached its present dominance by the mid-1960s; the other is the fact that the rise in public cynicism has been continuous through the same period even though there have been spells of good news as well as bad during the three decades. These two facts do not prove that television's portrayal of politics explains all the decline in confidence, but it is not unreasonable—especially in the light of Michael Robinson's 1968 study—to conclude that television has made a major contribution to that decline.

In my judgment, television has also played a significant role in several other developments that concern students of American political culture.

Television's Impact on Voting Turnout

Another recent trend in American political culture that has disturbed and puzzled a number of analysts is the steady decline in voting turnout in both presidential and congressional elections since 1960 (these figures are given in table 3.2). After all, most studies agree that the two factors most strongly correlated with nonvoting are low education and restrictive registration and voting laws.[22] Yet, the educational level of Americans has risen steadily and the restrictiveness of American registration and voting laws has lessened notably since the mid-1960s. Hence voting turnout should have increased in recent years, but it has not. Why?

Political analysts offer several explanations. Some say the decline has been produced largely by the "youthening" of the electorate between 1968 and 1972, when the minimum voting age was lowered from twenty-one to eighteen by the Twenty-Sixth Amendment to the Constitution.[23] Others point to the weakening of the voters' party loyalties (which we shall consider in chapter 4), and still others emphasize the decline in voters' feelings of "external political efficacy"—that is, their increasing tendency to believe that whatever they do, including voting, will have little influence on what government does.[24]

All these explanations are probably part of the story, but there is also considerable reason to believe (though no definitive proof) that television has made both a general and a special contribution to the decline of voting turnout. The general contribution arises from two facts: First, we have a great many elections in the United States, probably more than in any other modern democracy.[25] Second, television, as we shall note in detail in chapter 4, has now become by far the most important campaigning medium in contests for all major offices and many minor ones. The combination of the American "long

Television's Impact on American Political Culture

TABLE 3.2
Percentage of Voting Age Population Voting in Presidential and Congressional Elections, 1948–1982

	Percentage of Voting Age Population Voting for		
		House of Representatives	
Election Year	President	Presidential Years	Mid-Term Years
1948	51.1	48.1	
1950			41.1
1952	61.6	57.6	
1954			41.7
1956	59.3	55.9	
1958			43.0
1960	62.8	58.5	
1962			45.4
1964	61.9	57.8	
1966			45.4
1968	60.9	55.1	
1970			43.5
1972	55.5	50.9	
1974			36.1
1976	54.3	49.5	
1978			35.1
1980	53.2	48.1	
1982			35.7

SOURCES: For presidential elections, Paul R. Abramson, John H. Aldrich, and David W. Rohde, *Change and Continuity in the 1980 Election* (Washington, D.C.: Congressional Quarterly Press, 1982), Table 4–1, p. 78; for congressional elections, Norman J. Ornstein, Thomas E. Mann, Michael J. Malbin, and John F. Bibby, *Vital Statistics on Congress 1982* (Washington, D.C.: American Enterprise Institute, 1982), Table 1–1, p. 5. The figure for 1982 is taken from *Congressional Quarterly Weekly Report*, November 13, 1982, p. 2850.

ballot" and the dominance of television campaigning and news coverage inundates the voter with a flood of political advertisements, pictures of candidates campaigning, snippets from their speeches, it-is-it-isn't exchanges between the candidates, and the like. Given that many potential voters are already suspicious of and not much interested in politics, they may well conclude that these dozens of elections year after year simply cannot be as important as the candidates and newscasters try to make them seem—indeed, that perhaps they are not very important at all. Much research remains to be done before we can be sure how widespread and powerful is this general impact of television on nonvoting, but there does appear to be some fire behind the considerable body of smoke.

Some observers believe that the television networks make a special contribution to nonvoting by their early projections of the winners on election nights, sometimes well before the polls have closed and often after only 1 or 2 percent of the votes have been counted and reported. The network news chiefs deny that their projections have any such effect, and claim that their forecasts are in full compliance with the best standards of journalism. The argument is instructive and worth recounting in some detail.

In print journalism, scoops (reporting news before other papers do) are generally regarded as not only acceptable but one of the best ways of establishing a paper's superiority over its competitors. Hence newspapers have long tried to "call" election outcomes—that is, headline their projections of the winners—well before all the votes have been counted. And sometimes, inevitably, they have gotten it wrong, as in 1948 when the Chicago *Tribune* hit the streets early with its famous headline "Dewey Sweeps Nation," when in fact Harry Truman was the eventual winner.

To no one's surprise, radio and television newscasters have often tried for the same kind of scoops, and they have at least one enormous advantage over newspapers: they can put out new "editions" every few minutes, while newspapers can do so only every few hours. In recent years, moreover, the electronic media have developed several new techniques for calling election outcomes early that have left the newspapers far behind. One technique is the use of key precincts: the networks select several hundred precincts around the nation,

Television's Impact on American Political Culture

each typical of a certain important voting group (farmers, union labor, blacks, Jews, and the like). They develop for each precinct a "voting profile" of how it has voted in the past, and this provides a baseline of how each precinct would vote in a "normal" Democratic or Republican victory. They station reporters at each precinct to telephone its election results into network headquarters as soon as they are announced. The returns are fed into a high-speed computer, compared with the returns in past elections, and the network analysts can quickly tell whether a particular party's candidate is running well ahead or behind the average vote the party's winners have had in the past. On this basis they declare a particular candidate "elected" or "defeated," or the election "too close to call."

The newer, even more sophisticated technique is the "exit poll": the network stations interviewers at certain of its key precincts, and the interviewers stop a random sample of voters as they leave the polls, ask them how they voted and why, and telephone the results to the network headquarter's computer analysts. On this basis they have a strong indication of how the election is going to come out even before the polls close. And if a network's analysts have a clear indication from its exit polls that a particular candidate is sure to win, there is enormous pressure to scoop the other networks by announcing the projected winner first.

The television networks made election prediction right from their beginnings in the 1940s and 1950s; they began to use key precincts in the 1960s and "exit polls" in the 1970s. In 1960, both ABC and CBS called Richard Nixon the winner early on election night, but retracted their call later when it became clear that the race was eyelash close. In June 1964, CBS called Barry Goldwater the winner in the California Republican presidential primary while the polls were still open in the northern part of the state. Both episodes caused several bills to be introduced in Congress and in some state legislatures prohibiting such predictions while the polls were still open, but they got nowhere.

The issue came to the fore again in the 1980 election. On the basis of their exit polls, NBC's election team projected Ronald Reagan the winner in the presidential race at 8:15 P.M. EST and dramatized their scoop with "Reagan Wins" subtitles flashing at the bottom of their picture. At that time the polls were still open in one-third of the states in the Central time zone and in all the states in the zones further west. In California the polls were open another two hours and forty-five minutes after the NBC projection. At 9:50 P.M. EST, Jimmy Carter made his concession statement on national television even though the polls in California and other West Coast states were scheduled to remain open for another hour or more.

A new dimension was added to the controversy about the networks' projections the next day when it was learned that two prominent Democratic congressmen, James Corman of California and Al Ullman of Oregon, had unexpectedly lost by very narrow margins, and it was reported that many lines of voters in their districts had "melted away" after the NBC projection and the Carter concession.[26]

This touched off yet another round of complaints against the networks and bills were introduced in Congress and some state legislatures to prohibit the election-night broadcasting of election outcome projections before all the polls have closed and/or to have all polls close at the same real time. The issues involved have been discussed at length elsewhere,[27] and the key questions appear to be the following.

First, do the early projections in fact discourage some people from voting who otherwise would vote? The first studies of this question focused mainly on early projections of the 1964 presidential election, and they found no statistically significant impact on voting turnout. In defending their early projections ever since, the network news chiefs have relied heavily upon

Television's Impact on American Political Culture

these findings. However, the 1964 studies were all based upon very small numbers of potentially susceptible voters in the Western states and had other methodological flaws as well. Wolfinger and Linquiti sought to remedy these shortcomings by studying the 1972 elections, using data from a very large Census Bureau sample. They found an estimated drop of 2.7 percent in turnout in the West for which there was no plausible explanation other than the networks' early projections of a Nixon landslide; but their study too has been criticized on technical grounds.[28] Most recently, a study by John E. Jackson, using data from the 1980 national election study by the Center for Political Studies of the University of Michigan, reports a significant decline in voting in the Western states as a direct result of the early projections of the Reagan landslide.[29]

What are we to make of this welter of conflicting findings? The fairest conclusion, I believe, is that, while there is as yet no definitive proof that the early projections lower voting turnout, there is enough reason to believe that they might to ask the question of what, if anything, can and should be done about it.

The second question, then, is how can even the possibility of such an effect be eliminated? Many suggestions have been made, and some are embodied in the various provisions of proposed legislation. They include flat legal prohibitions against broadcasting election outcome projections until all the polls have closed; making polling hours in all jurisdictions the same in real time; voluntary restraint by the networks; and private boycotts of the networks' exit polls to force restraint on them.[30]

The final question is what social benefits, if any, do the networks' early projections provide? What would we lose if they were somehow curtailed or eliminated, other than our present ability to go to bed early on election night because we know already who is going to win? Many of the networks' critics agree with Elizabeth Byerly of the League of Women

85

Voters that "no useful purpose [is] served by these projections, no value to counter their potential for affecting, not just reporting, election results."[31]

The network news chiefs, on the other hand, claim that the projections not only do no harm but are in full accord with the highest canons of journalism. As William A. Leonard, then president of CBS News, put it before a congressional committee in 1981:

> We believe our responsibility is that of any news organization: to report accurately the information we have, and its significance, as soon as it becomes available. That is nothing unique to election reporting; with the rarest exceptions, it is a fundamental journalist credo. We cannot patronize our audience by withholding from them what we know. To do so would be a violation of trust and would seriously jeopardize our credibility.[32]

Conclusion

Whether one agrees or disagrees with either or both, the Byerly and Leonard statements just quoted provide clear and striking examples of the very different views held by television newspeople and some of their critics about the medium's cultural impact and social responsibilities.

The controversy over the networks' election night early projections is likely to continue for some time. Yet I believe it is now well established that television's special way of presenting political news and information has had a powerful impact on American political culture. To be sure, it has not, all by itself, transformed that culture into something entirely different from what it was before the television age. But it has altered the culture significantly by intensifying ordinary Americans' traditional low opinion of politics and politicians, by exacerbating the decline in their trust and confidence in their

Television's Impact on American Political Culture

government and its institutions, and by helping to make them even less inclined to vote than they used to be.

Perhaps, as many television newspeople would argue, their political reporting has helped to remove the scales from ordinary Americans' eyes about what really goes on behind the closed doors of Washington (and Albany and Sacramento) and thereby provided the necessary basis for cleaning up its more unsavory aspects. Perhaps so, and perhaps the benefit has been worth the cost. Perhaps not.

Sideline commentators like me can analyze and applaud or deplore this political culture shaped in good part by television, but few think it is going to go away or even change very much. However, for the politicians and political organizations that are, or want to be, on the field playing the game, it is a fact of life. Like it or not, the political culture constitutes the setting and provides many of the constraints within which politicians must operate. How it affects them and how they try to use it for their own purposes are the main concerns of the next chapter.

Chapter 4

Television's Impact on American Politicians

IN 1979, I attended a conference of political scientists and politicians on the subject of what is happening to our political parties. As we usually do on such occasions, the political scientists soon fell to arguing heatedly about what had been the effects of the many reforms made in the presidential nominating process since 1968 and even more heatedly about what further reforms, if any, should be made.[1]

After awhile, John Sears, who was then, as in 1976, director of Ronald Reagan's campaign for the Republican presidential nomination,[2] felt compelled to say a word for the politicians. "You political scientists should understand," he said, "that no matter what set of rules you fellows or the government come up with, we politicians will have to live with them and try to figure ways of turning them to our advantage. But it would be helpful if everyone would leave the present rules, good or bad, alone for awhile so that we can get used to them and learn how to work with them."

Television's Impact on American Politicians

That struck some of us as a voice of common sense from the real world, and we subsided for a time, though not, of course, permanently. But Sears's basic point is important for understanding the topic of this book: "Changing the rules changes the game," as William Cavala put it so tellingly;[3] and in the United States since World War II we have been changing the rules of the game of politics more radically than at any time since the Progressive era early in this century.

It is equally true, however, that changing the environment also changes the game. And the basic argument of this book is that the advent of television as the principal source of political reality for most Americans has altered the political game profoundly, perhaps more profoundly than all the parties' rules changes and new state and federal laws put together. It has had an enormous impact on the kinds of persons who become successful politicians and on how they conduct their business. Even so, we sometimes overlook the fact that the relationship between television and the politicians is a two-way street—that politicians, in the manner described by John Sears, are not supine victims of the television age; rather they seek to understand its constraints and opportunities and to turn them to their own advantage if they can.

Accordingly, the purposes of this chapter are to detail some of the consequences of the television age for American politicians and to describe some of the ways in which they try to use television for their own ends.

Changes in Electoral Politics

The most obvious, though not necessarily the most important, respect in which television has changed the politician's world is its impact on electoral politics, both in the ways in which campaigns are conducted and in the kinds of candidates who do best under the camera's eye.

THE CONDUCT OF CAMPAIGNS

Politicians have long believed that face-to-face contact between politicians and voters is by far the most effective way to campaign.[4] Many no doubt still believe it, but they all recognize that in the 1980s' world of mass constituencies and of voters who would rather stay home and watch television than attend a political rally in some auditorium, appearing on television is the closest candidates can get to all but a handful of their constituents and provides by far the most cost-effective campaigning device they have. Moreover, appearing on television is almost as good as appearing in person: politicians generally believe, with Kurt and Gladys Lang, that watching something on television makes people think "that they 'see for themselves,' that they are directly involved in history, that television takes them to the scene. . . . , that they have a clearer picture of what is going on than people right 'there.'"[5] Put another way, while eye-to-eye contact and a warm handshake between politician and voter may be best, having the politician's voice and face appear in living color on the tube a few feet away from the constituent in his own living room is surely second best.

There are, of course, two forms of campaign television: "paid television," in which the campaign organization produces the equivalent of a commercial advertisement and pays the stations and networks to air them; and "free television," in which the broadcasters find what the candidate is doing and saying sufficiently interesting and newsworthy for them to broadcast it as part of their public affairs coverage in newscasts and interview slots in magazine shows. Both forms are vital to any well-run campaign in a large (national or statewide) constituency, but free television is generally thought to

Television's Impact on American Politicians

be the more desirable of the two, and not for budgetary reasons alone. As Larry Sabato puts it:

> Paid media gives certainty of control and flexibility, but it cannot match the unpaid media for credibility or, in most cases, for size and attentiveness of audience. The three networks' evening news now reaches an average of 28 million homes. The average local station, copying the national networks, is devoting more time to public affairs programs and hiring a far larger news staff. All political consultants fully acknowledge that the unpaid media, more than paid media, can make or break a candidate.[6]

One result, according to Robert Agranoff, is that "the campaign must be planned and organized around the media schedule. The event to be covered must meet the news deadline of the radio and TV stations."[7] Another is that every campaign organization must have at least one (many have more) "media director" who is skilled at mounting and scheduling campaign events that will get maximum exposure on free television. This is a technical skill requiring both talent and experience, and people who have these skills usually sell them to campaign organizations for large fees. The same can be said for the professionals who manage the many other technical operations of modern campaigns, such as taking and analyzing public opinion polls, compiling computerized mailing lists of potential supporters and donors and sending them direct mail appeals, producing and purchasing time for televised political advertisements, and the like.

There are, indeed, so many and varied technical skills needed to run a modern large-scale, television-centered campaign that the greatest need of all is for someone at the top to develop the strategy and tactics, to use them to the best advantage, and to coordinate all the technical specialists behind the master plan. Hardly any candidates or leaders of the parties' state or county organizations have the necessary technical know-how to do the top job, and so there has arisen a whole new profession of political consultants who have taken over the direction of most major campaigns. Some will work only for Democratic or Republican or liberal or conservative candidates, but more are "hired guns" who will work for any candidate who will pay their fees. Almost all of them, however, have in common the fact that their prepolitical experience has been in the fields of advertising and public relations, both heavily dependent on using the mass media, and not in the organizations and activities of political parties. A comprehensive list of the most successful political consultants would be far too long to publish here, but any such list would certainly include the names of Douglas Bailey, John Deardourff, David Garth, Joseph Napolitan, Matt Reese, and Stuart Spencer.

The point to note is that political consultants have also entirely replaced party politicians as the top organizers and strategists of large-scale political campaigns.[8] That is a logical and probably inevitable consequence of the growing dominance of television in campaigning that, according to Anthony Smith, has taken place not only in the United States but in all Western-style democracies:

> Even before the microphone, the politician aimed his words through the crowd, not at it: his real target was the reporters' bench and the rows of shorthand books. The microphone made the politician aware of the vastness of the political space in which he operated and of the invisible audience to which he had to project himself. For a century the stuff of politics was tailored to the needs of the newspaper, and until a generation ago the newspaper was shaped by the requirements of politics. Out of the connection came a symbolic system of communication: the newspapers described debates, conflicts, demonstrations, activities. The innovation of television was actually to show personalities and events: to a large degree, the television coverage *is* the electoral campaign.[9]

PROCESS OF SELECTING CANDIDATES

Many political scientists, including me, believe that selecting candidates is the heart of the electoral process, for it sets

Television's Impact on American Politicians

the final choices for the voters and, in the process, eliminates far more potential officeholders than do the final contests between the major parties' nominees. Since the early 1900s, the United States has been the only country in the world to choose most of its candidates by the direct primary system, in which anyone can enter the contest for a party's nomination and the selection is made, not, as in most other democracies, by small groups of party leaders, but by ordinary voters who have designated themselves as party members.[10]

The old Progressives were the principal architects of the direct primary. They intended the system to transfer the power to choose candidates from the party bosses to ordinary people and thereby to give "outsider" and "independent" aspirants a chance to win office. By and large the system has achieved those objectives, although some observers feel that it has, in the process, contributed heavily to the weakening of the parties.[11]

Be that as it may, the direct primary means that campaigns directed at ordinary voters are, if anything, even more important in primary elections than in general elections. In general elections, after all, the candidates are labeled on the ballots as "Democrats" or "Republicans"; and while those labels may not be as important in the 1980s as they were in the 1950s, for many Americans they are still important cues for distinguishing the good guys from the bad guys. But there are no such labels and cues in primary elections, only a list of names. In such an unstructured situation even the elementary matter of name recognition becomes crucial: other things being equal, people will prefer an aspirant they have at least heard of to a complete unknown.

That simple fact has probably made television's impact on campaigning even greater in primary elections than in general elections, for no other campaigning method can match a series of well-produced and widely-broadcast series of paid television advertisements and, even better, frequent unpaid appear-

93

ances on newscasts and interviews, to make a particular aspirant emerge triumphant from a pack of unknowns.

While the advent of television has had a major impact on selecting candidates for all large-constituency offices, its most visible and most-studied impact has been on the campaigns of aspirants for the major parties' presidential nominations. The rules of that particular political game have changed radically in the past two decades. In 1968 and before, only about one-third of the delegates to each party's convention were chosen or bound by primaries, and the other two-thirds were chosen by small groups of party leaders meeting in state conventions, state committees, or even governors' offices. Since 1968, however, more and more states have been adding presidential primaries. The result has been that in 1980 nearly three-quarters of the delegates to the national conventions were chosen by primaries, most of them pledged to vote for a particular aspirant until he released them.

The consequence is that the national conventions have become to the nominating process approximately what the Electoral College is to the electing process: they no longer *make* decisions on their own; they *register* decisions made by the persons voting in the primaries weeks and months before the conventions meet. So the primaries, much more than the conventions, are where the real action takes place.

Presidential primaries, let us remember, are mass elections. In 1980, they involved a total of over 32 million voters. So they necessarily require mass campaigns rather than maneuvering in smoke-filled rooms. And in any kind of mass campaign television is bound to play a critical role in deciding the winners.

For one thing, the networks' newscast producers' decisions that particular aspirants are not important enough to be worth covering in itself effectively eliminates them from the race.[12]

For another thing, the primaries are held, not all at once, but *sequentially* over a period of months.[13] For some time now the

Television's Impact on American Politicians

press and the television networks have covered the early primaries (especially those in New Hampshire, Massachusets, Florida, Illinois, Wisconsin, and Pennsylvania) far more intensively than the later primaries despite the fact that the early primaries together choose only about one-third of all the delegates. For example, Michael Robinson's study of coverage of the 1976 primaries found the following:

> New Hampshire, which gave Carter his first primary victory, cast a total of 82,381 Democratic votes. On the day following the election, the New Hampshire results received 2,100 seconds of total news time on the three networks—an average of 700 news seconds per network. New York, which was [Senator Henry] Jackson's biggest victory, cast 3,746,414 Democratic votes. On the following day, his victory received only 560 seconds on the three shows combined—fewer than 190 seconds per network. Thus the New Hampshire results received 170 times as much network news time per Democratic vote as the outcome in New York.[14]

The result is what politicians call the "frontloading" of the presidential candidate selection process: the candidates who do best in the early primaries are described by the networks and the print press as the "frontrunners" who hold "commanding leads." The benefits of this early position are many. The frontrunners, no matter how far behind they started, rise rapidly in the public opinion polls, and they find it much easier to raise money and enlist volunteers. Their opponents sink in the polls, find it harder to attract money and workers, and often drop out or "discontinue active campaigning."

Momentum in Presidential Nominations. Doing best in the early primaries is not simply a matter of getting more votes than the other candidates; it is getting substantially more votes "than expected." Query: expected by whom? Answer: by the analysts of the press and the networks. For example, in the 1972 New Hampshire Democratic primary, Edmund Muskie ran first with 46 percent of the votes and George McGovern ran second with 37 percent. But the media had previously

95

announced that Muskie was expected (by them) to get well over 50 percent and McGovern was expected to get only 25 percent. Consequently, the networks' big story on election night was not "Muskie wins by nine points," but "surprisingly strong showing by McGovern." From then on Muskie went down in the polls and McGovern went up, Muskie eventually withdrew, and McGovern won the nomination.

The Democratic contest of 1976 provided an even more impressive example of media-generated momentum.[15] Jimmy Carter began his drive for the presidential nomination in 1974 not only as an outsider but as an almost total unknown.[16] But his underdog's strategy was among the best ever formulated, and its success remains one of the greatest achievements in the history of American electoral politics.

Carter began active campaigning in Iowa and New Hampshire over a year before the scheduled contests, and his plan was to parlay early successes there into at least serious-candidate status and perhaps even frontrunner status, on the ground that the growing momentum could, in turn, be parlayed into the nomination.

It was a brilliant plan, it was executed superbly, and it succeeded famously against great initial odds. The course of its triumph can be divided into three stages. Stage one began with Carter's win in the January 19 Iowa precinct caucuses. Delegates pledged to him won only 28 percent of the votes, compared with 37 percent for "uncommitted" delegates; but he more than doubled Birch Bayh's 13 percent, Fred Harris's 10 percent, and Morris Udall's 6 percent. The news media barely mentioned the high uncommitted vote (after all, "uncommitted" was certainly not going to be the nominee), and Walter Cronkite spoke for just about all of the pundits when he said on the "CBS Evening News" the next night, "The Iowa voters have spoken, and for the Democrats what they said was 'Jimmy Carter.'" Then came caucuses in Mississippi,

Television's Impact on American Politicians

Maine, and Oklahoma, with mixed results for Carter, but they received very little media attention.

The second big campaign event, as in 1972, was the February 24 New Hampshire primary. Again Carter's early, sustained, and intensive campaigning paid off with a modest electoral plurality and a big media victory. He won 28 percent of the vote, there was no centrist to challenge him, and the four liberals (Udall, Bayh, Harris, and Sargent Shriver) together received 57 percent but divided it among themselves so that Udall's 23 percent was the largest single share. The media now declared that Carter was the front runner. His new status was further enhanced by his win over George Wallace in the March 9 Florida primary and his eyelash win over Udall in the April 6 Wisconsin primary (after two networks had projected Udall to be the winner). His momentum was not significantly slowed by Henry Jackson's wins in the March 2 Massachusetts primary and the difficult-to-report April 6 New York primary. And his frontrunner position was clinched, and perhaps the ultimate nomination as well, by his winning the April 27 Pennsylvania primary with 37 percent to Jackson's 19 percent. At the end of stage one in April, only 39 percent of all the primary votes that eventually would be cast had actually been cast, and Carter had won only 38 percent of those cast. Only 38 percent of all the delegates to be selected had actually been selected, and Carter had won only 29 percent of those that had been selected. Nevertheless, the media all but unanimously agreed that Carter had built up a "commanding lead" and, "barring a miracle," would win the nomination.

Stage two featured challenges to Carter from two late-entering candidates, Frank Church and Jerry Brown. There were sixteen primaries from May 4 to June 1, and Carter entered fifteen, while Brown entered five and Church eight. It is worth remembering that Carter won all eight of the primaries in which neither Church nor Brown was entered, and finished second in six of the eight contested by one or both of his new rivals. But momentum is evidently much harder to achieve or lose in the middle of the campaign that at its beginning, for Carter's mediocre performance in stage two did not appreciably damage his chances for the nomination. Church and Brown demonstrated repeatedly that Carter could be beaten in primaries, but the media did not even speculate about whether either of them could actually win the nomination. When stage two concluded with little-noticed June 1 wins for Church (Montana), Brown (Rhode Island), and Carter (South Dakota), the contest was over two-thirds completed. Of all the primary votes that were eventually cast, 69 percent had now been cast, and Carter's 42.5 percent of those votes was far ahead of any other candidate's share. Also, 2,253 of the ultimate 3,003 delegates (75 percent) had been chosen, and 869 (38.6 percent) were committed to Carter—again, far more than to any other candidate.

At the beginning of stage three in early June, there were still a few speculations in the press that the anti-Carter forces might yet combine to stop him and a deadlocked convention might turn to Hubert Humphrey. But on June 5 Chicago's Mayor Richard J. Daley, back at the center of the nominating process from which the McGovernites had excluded him in 1972, announced that the convention should not hand the nomination to anyone who had not sought the people's approval in the primaries (obviously referring to Humphrey), and he added that if Carter won the June 8 Ohio primary (which the polls showed he was likely to do) he was sure to win the nomination. On June 8, Carter was crushed by Brown in California with 20 percent to Brown's 59 percent, but he won Ohio with 52 percent to Udall's 21 percent and Church's 14 percent. The game was over. All the other candidates except Brown endorsed Carter, and by mid-June he had the nomination all locked up—the earliest it had been locked up by a nonincumbent candidate in either party since Alfred M.

Television's Impact on American Politicians

Landon won the Republican nomination in 1936. Most observers agreed that Carter's early momentum, created largely by the way the press and the networks reported the results and significance of the Iowa caucuses and the New Hampshire primary months earlier, were the prime causes of his astonishing victory.[17]

The National Conventions. Now that they no longer choose the candidates, the national party conventions have become almost entirely spectacles for television. The story of how this came about is instructive.

From the 1830s to the 1920s the preconvention campaigns of presidential aspirants were, by modern standards, very small scale, and what little activity took place was barely mentioned in the newspapers. The conventions were usually reported fairly widely by the major newspapers, although most of the coverage consisted of summary stories published after the conventions had adjourned.

The advent of radio in the 1920s radically changed all that. In 1924, many of the burgeoning radio stations broadcast frequent news bulletins from the wire services about what was going on in the conventions, especially in the Democrats' 103-ballot contest in Philadelphia. In 1928, some stations began live broadcasting of the conventions' proceedings, and by 1936 over 200 stations were broadcasting part or all of the conventions' proceedings.[18]

The first telecast of a convention was made on a small scale in 1940 and perhaps it was more coincidental than significant that the Republican convention that year nominated Wendell L. Willkie, who remains Jimmy Carter's only rival for the distinction of being the most "outsider" candidate ever nominated by a major party.[19] By 1952, as we have seen, television had become more than a laboratory curiosity, and it had a significant impact on the 1952 conventions. Both parties had originally decided to meet in the Chicago Stadium, but when the networks complained that the arena's cramped space left too little room for their bulky cameras and lights, the parties agreed to switch to Chicago's International Amphitheater (an arena built near the stockyards for animal shows, but with plenty of room for the delegates and the television crews and equipment).

In 1956, for the first time, both parties designed their physical arrangements and their convention schedules so as to look good on prime-time television; for example, they interspersed the politicians' speeches with frequent performances by professional singers and orchestras.

Since then the conventions have been broadcast live by the networks ("gavel-to-gavel" by CBS and NBC, although ABC in 1976 and 1980 broadcast only summaries and highlights of each day). In 1980, the networks together spent about $30 million and used over 1,800 people to cover the conventions, and both parties did their best to conduct their proceedings so as to provide the best possible show for the millions of viewers: for example, they occasionally darkened the auditorium and showed professionally-made films extolling the parties and their leaders.

In some respects, though, the television newspeople were more of a show than the people and events they reported. The anchors and commentators sat behind large desks in huge transparent booths high above the conventions' floors, looking down, like gods, on the antics of the politicians milling about below. When the famous reporters, such as Dan Rather, Tom Brokaw, Barbara Walters, and Judy Woodruff, appeared on the floor to interview delegates they invariable attracted large crowds, and many delegates asked for their autographs.

The full importance of television's presence became apparent at the Republican convention in Detroit during the complicated negotiations between the presidential nominee, Ronald Reagan, and former president Gerald R. Ford over whether Ford would be willing to run for vice-president on the Reagan

Television's Impact on American Politicians

ticket. At the most delicate moment of the negotiations, Ford gave an interview to CBS's Walter Cronkite in which he was interpreted as saying that there was a real chance that something could be worked out. Ford's "going public" in this manner forced Reagan's hand earlier than he would have preferred; a few hours later he went before the convention and announced that his choice for the vice-presidential nominee was George Bush.[20]

George Comstock sums up very well what television has done to the national conventions:

> Television has changed the nominating conventions from deliberative, if volatile, bodies to orchestrated showcases. This has come about in several ways. By opening the conventions to the television viewer, politicians have become fearful of offending anyone by what transpires. The function of television as entertainment cannot be ignored, as the parties wish to hold as many viewers as possible for the display of the nominee and his running mate. Inoffensive, contrived excitement is packaged. When that is what the parties offer, television can only conspire in its transmission in as dramatic a manner as possible, for the medium shares a goal with the party—a large, attentive audience.
>
> The transformation has been hastened by what television has done to the primaries and by the journalistic machinery assembled by television for convention coverage. By focusing attention on the primaries as if each were *High Noon* again and again, the role of negotiation among party leaders in selecting a candidate has been reduced. For delegates and leaders alike less remains to be decided or bargained for at the conventions.[21]

THE SUCCESSFUL CANDIDATES

If changing the rules changes the game, then every change of rules is likely to help some kinds of players and handicap others. Certainly the central role television has come to play in the game of mass-election politics has helped candidates who can afford to hire the very best in political consultants, media specialists, makeup artists, and prime-time exposure. But has it also given special advantages to candidates with other assets than money?

There is, as yet, no definitive answer to that question. However, many observers of television-age American politics have given their impressions, and they almost all agree that being "good on television" has become one of the first requirements (some say *the* first) for being a successful candidate for nomination and election to the presidency, a governorship, a seat in the U.S. Senate, or any office with a constituency that encompasses one or more television markets.

So much seems sensible, perhaps obvious. But what makes one aspirant good on television and another not so good? Some social science mass communications theory suggests some clues.

A "Cool" Medium? Still the best known (though not best understood) of the modern mass communications theorists is the late Marshall McLuhan. One of his most familiar ideas is that television is a "cool" medium that, in politics, advantages "cool" candidates and handicaps "hot" ones. McLuhan defined the two categories thus:

> There is a basic principle that distinguishes . . . a hot medium like the movie from a cool one like TV. A hot medium is one that extends one single sense in "high definition." High definition is the state of being well filled with data. A photograph is, visually, "high definition." A cartoon is "low definition," simply because very little visual information is provided. . . . Hot media are, therefore, low in participation, and cool media are high in participation or completion by the audience.[22]

McLuhan argued from this premise that television is a cool medium because its pictures are of low definition compared with movies and photographs, its sound is of much lower fidelity than most radio and records, and all in all it leaves a good deal for the viewer to fill in. In politics, he continued,

Television's Impact on American Politicians

television is very hard on candidates with "hot" personalities, such as Senator Joseph McCarthy or Richard Nixon (McLuhan's illustrations). They both presented very strong and sharply defined partisan images, leaving few blank spaces for the viewers to fill in with their own issue and personality preferences.[23]

Favoring "Cool" Candidates? Some of McLuhan's successors have recast his argument by saying that television favors the candidates who come over the tube as "nice guys" over the ones who impress viewers as "strong partisans" or "tough advocates." Most observers agree that the kind of personality, appearance, and speaking style that inspires standing ovations from crowds of thousands in auditoriums is quite different from the kind that inspires liking and confidence from a few people sitting in front of a television set in their own homes. The auditorium situation calls for a commanding presence, a strong voice projected at a high volume, large gestures, and dramatic punch lines with plenty of pauses for cheers. The TV-room situation calls for a pleasant and friendly presence, a moderate tone of voice, small and natural gestures, and a general conversational manner. Tony Schwartz, one of the most successful of the political media specialists, puts it this way:

> In assessing the reactions of voters to candidates on television, it becomes very clear that a person sitting in his home watching a political figure on his TV set four or five feet away wants to feel that the candidate is talking to him. A politician who typically speaks to large audiences, in a grandiose style, must adjust his speech scale for television or radio. Though he may be part of an audience totaling 10 or 20 million people, a TV viewer experiences the candidate as someone speaking in his home to one, two, or maybe five people gathered around the set.[24]

There surely is something in this, even though we cannot yet be scientifically precise about just what it is. It is tempting, for instance, to explain in these terms a good deal of John

Connally's thundering failure in the 1980 race for the Republican presidential nomination. In many respects Connally seemed at the outset to be a formidable candidate. He had held high office in both Democratic and Republican administrations and had been governor of a major state. He was tall, handsome, and had a commanding presence: many people said of him, "He *looks* like a president." And he had a great deal of money to spend. Most observers thought he was the greatest stump speaker in the field, and in one large auditorium after another he consistently brought crowds of thousands to their feet in cheering, stamping ovations. On the other hand, his major competition, Ronald Reagan, was an aging ex-movie and television star who generally pleased rather than inspired the people he talked to.

Connally decided that the best way to capitalize on his considerable assets was to save his first major effort for the South Carolina primary in March 1980, where he had the active support of the state's most powerful Republican, Senator Strom Thurmond. He reportedly spent about $11.5 million, mostly on televised advertisements and speeches, much of it in South Carolina. Yet in the primary he won only 30 percent of the votes to Reagan's 55 percent, and withdrew from the race. All his efforts and his $11.5 million had won him exactly one delegate, probably the most expensive delegate in the history of presidential politics.

Why did Connally fail so disastrously? No doubt there were many reasons, but surely one was the fact that Connally's "hot" speaking style that was so enormously successful in his auditorium speeches did not come across well over the "cool" medium of television in the homes of South Carolina (and Iowa and New Hampshire).[25]

However one may explain Connally's problems, it is hard to reject the belief widely held by political consultants that in today's political world candidates who are not good on television will have to have great advantages in all other respects to

Television's Impact on American Politicians

overcome such a crippling handicap. What impact this may have on the quality and role perceptions of our elected public officials is discussed in chapter 5.

Changes in Political Parties

Just about everyone recognizes that, with the exception of a few brief episodes, America's national political parties have not been cohesive and powerful policy-making agencies of government, especially when compared with the major parties in other democratic countries.[26] In this sense they are certainly "weak" in the 1980s, but no weaker than at most times in the past.

In some other aspects, however, the major parties during most of American history have performed a number of functions of great importance for our politico-governmental system, and in those respects at least they have been very strong elements of that system. At least until the 1970s most of the textbooks emphasized the national parties' leading role in at least five functions.[27]

First and foremost, in their congressional caucuses and their national delegate conventions they chose the only presidential candidates who had serious chances of being elected, and thereby provided the voters with meaningful and manageable choices. They more than any other agency democratized the selection of the president.

Second, they were the principal money raisers for, and organizers of, presidential campaigns, and thereby provided the main stimuli for getting ordinary citizens to take an interest in politics and vote.

Third, by inspiring "party identifications" in most people they provided the main cognitive sorting devices that enabled ordinary people to make sense out of politics and furnished them with a meaningful basis for voting on a wide variety of offices and in the frequent elections the American "long ballot" dumps on its citizens.[28]

Fourth, they constituted the only organizations both large enough and with broad enough goals to take the demands of the many special-interest groups, moderate them, and meld them into general programs the nation could live with.[29]

Finally, because they performed all these functions where no other institution did or could, the national parties provided the main moderating and unifying force that held together a variegated people and a fragmented governmental system and made them work.[30]

In short, prior to the 1970s most commentators believed that, although America's national parties were far weaker than their European counterparts as agencies for formulating and executing government programs, they were very strong as makers of nominations, organizers and financers of campaigns, and introducers of sense and order in the confusing world of politics so that ordinary people could understand and deal with it. Without them, the system would work very badly or not at all.

THE POST-1960S DECLINE

Today, however, most observers believe that in most of these respects the parties have weakened significantly since the late 1960s, and some say that party "dealignment" has gone so far that in national politics in the 1980s we now have something closely approaching a no-party system.[31] According to this view, the leading manifestations of the parties' decline are the following:

1. Declining party identifications. Every two years since 1952, the Center for Political Studies at the University of Michigan has been

Television's Impact on American Politicians

asking national samples of adult Americans about the nature and intensity of their party identifications. The results from 1960 to 1980 are shown in table 4.1.

TABLE 4.1
Intensities of American Party Identifications, 1960–1980

Year	Party Identifiers Strong	Party Identifiers Weak	Independents Leaning to a Party (percentages)	Independents Not Leaning	Apolitical, Don't Know
1960	35	38	15	8	4
1964	38	38	14	8	2
1968	30	39	18	11	2
1972	25	39	21	13	2
1976	24	39	22	14	1
1980	27	37	21	13	2

SOURCE: Adapted from Samuel J. Eldersveld, *Political Parties in American Society* (New York: Basic Books, 1982), Table 4.2, p. 76.

The figures in table 4.1 show that Americans' party identifications were at their most intense in 1964, dropped sharply in 1968, and leveled off at a substantially lower point in 1976 and 1980. In 1980, 37 percent of the people considered themselves weak identifiers with one of the parties, 21 percent were independents who to some degree leaned toward one of the parties, and only 27 percent felt they were strong partisans—compared with the 38 percent who had felt that way in 1964. So there is little doubt that substantially fewer Americans feel strongly attached to a political party in the 1980s than was the case in the 1950s and 1960s.

2. Declining role in choosing presidential nominees. We have already reviewed this development.
3. Declining roles in raising money for and directing presidential campaigns. We have also reviewed this development.
4. Declining ability to resist, moderate, or meld the demands of special-interest groups. In 1978 Meg Greenfield, editorial page editor of the *Washington Post* wrote:

> I can't remember a time in Washington when interest-group issues and politics so dominated events. And every day the units

107

of protest and concern seem to be subdividing into even smaller and more specialized groupings.... By now, there can hardly be a cultural, racial, regional, economic or professional group for whom the lawmakers in Washington have not fashioned some special statutory blessing—a prerogative, a grant, an exemption, a reimbursement.... something. It puts a premium on identifying yourself with the special subgroup and helps to thin, if not destroy, whatever feelings of larger national loyalty various citizens may have.[32]

Few Washington-watchers would dispute the accuracy of her observations, and many would add that the most important single cause for this sad state of affairs is the weakening of the political parties.

A few observers dispute this widely-held decline-of-the-parties thesis. They say that actually only the Democrats have declined, while the Republicans have not only kept their identifiers as loyal as ever but have substantially increased the activity and strength of their national organizations, particularly the Republican National Committee, the Republican Congressional Campaign Committee, and the Republican Senatorial Campaign Committee. They point to the great success these organizations have had since the mid-1970s in recruiting good candidates for Congress and the state legislatures, in holding national schools on campaign organization and techniques for candidates, in raising millions of dollars to spend on national advertising, and on helping Republican candidates throughout the country in developing a sophisticated and remunerative direct-mail system for fundraising, and so on.[33]

There is some truth to this, and yet even the strong, rich, and active Republican National Committee plays every bit as minor a role in choosing Republican presidential nominees and directing presidential campaigns as the Democratic National Committee plays in Democratic nominations and campaigns. And Michael Malbin's account of platform making in the two parties' 1980 conventions suggests that the Republicans were only a little more successful than the Democrats in resisting or moderating the power of interest groups to get their maximum demands written into their platform.[34] Accordingly, whatever may be the current differences between the operations and intraparty influence of the Republicans' and Democrats' national organizations, it still is apparent that the two parties taken together play considerably less significant roles than they did before World War II in the minds of the voters, in the choice of presidential candidates, in the financing and directing of presidential campaigns, and in the moderation and melding of special-interest group demands. If that is the case, it becomes appropriate to ask why the parties have declined in these respects.

THE CAUSES

Most of the people who believe that the parties have declined do not blame (or credit) any single social development as *the* cause. Some, like me, have emphasized the parties' own rules changes, particularly the Democrats' post-1969 rules for selecting national convention delegates, including such measures as quotas for women, blacks, and other minority groups, proportional representation in the allocation of the delegates reflecting the candidates' shares of the votes in presidential primaries, and abolition of guaranteed delegate status for party leaders.[35]

Others have stressed the proliferation of presidential primaries: in 1968, seventeen states held such primaries, which chose about 35 percent of the national conventions' delegates; in 1980, thirty-five states held primaries, which chose about 74 percent of the delegates.[36]

Still others have focused mainly on the new laws, especially the amendments to the Federal Election Campaign Act in 1974, regulating the financing of campaigns for presidential nominations and elections, which, they say, have almost eliminated the parties as significant money raisers in presidential politics and left the field to public financing, the ad hoc candidate organizations, and the PACs (political action committees).[37]

Yet others have pointed to such more general social developments as the population's increased level of formal education in public school systems that often teach vote-for-the-person-not-the-party as the essence of good citizenship; the decline in the respectability of material gain as a motive for participating in politics; the growing dominance of the parties by "purist" political activists, who are mainly concerned with ideological purity, and the corresponding decline of the old-style party organization faithful who cared mainly about putting together coalitions to win elections.[38]

A convincing case can be made for each of the foregoing as a cause for the national parties' decline, and they all seem to have played a greater or lesser part. But some commentators have argued that an even greater cause for the decline has been the "televisation" of our national politics.

As we observed in chapter 2, television's built-in need for "good visuals," novelty, and continuing story lines in its newscasts, combined with the neo-progressive framework within which the producers, correspondents, and anchors of network news receive and purvey political information, has made television focus on personalities, not organizations, and certainly not old-hat, slightly smelly organizations like political parties.[39] This surely has contributed to their lower significance in many people's minds, although we cannot say that it is the sole or even the most important cause of the decline in strong party identifications.

More important is the fact that television has, in fact if not intention, preempted many of the parties' traditional functions. As we noted earlier, parties used to be the nation's principal agencies for testing and screening presidential aspirants, for choosing presidential candidates, for conducting and financing presidential campaigns, and for stimulating popular interest and participation in politics. But we have also seen that the proliferation of the presidential primaries has transferred the selection of presidential candidates from the party leaders to the people who vote in the primaries, and that, combined with the advent of television as the main source of information about candidates and issues for those voters, has effectively shifted the candidate-screening process from the parties to the television news services.[40]

Also relevant is the fact that many of the political consultants who have taken over the management of campaigns from the party politicians not only ignore the parties but are downright hostile to them. Larry Sabato reports:

> Most political consultants are at least passively hostile to the parties, the more ideological among them, contemptuous. At times consultants can sound like the evangelical populists they often portray their candidates to be, railing against the evils of boss rule. "Really the only major function of the political party structure these days is to nominate the candidates for president, and my personal feeling is that we'd all be better off if this responsibility also were placed in the hands of the people," Joe Napolitan has written. Bob Goodman, in tones echoed time and again by his fellow independent professionals, lauds consultants for unshackling candidates, putting them beyond the reach of the petty party barons:

And Sabato quotes Goodman as saying:

> We have enabled people to come into a party or call themselves independent Democrats or Republicans and run for office without having to pay the dues of being a party member in a feudal way. Meaning kiss the ass of certain people and maybe down the line they'll give you a shot at public office.[41]

Many consultants, indeed, have adopted the strategy of running their candidates with little or no mention of their party labels, and often they run them *against* their parties' "bosses" and "machines," stressing their "independence" and absence of any debts to any party organization or leader. This strategy is often highly successful—witness the case of Jimmy Carter in 1976[42]—and the adverse effect it has had on the parties as institutions is either shrugged off or welcomed.

It should be stressed that none of this is unique to the United States. In his comparative analysis of what has happened in twenty-eight democratic countries, in all of which a political communications system once dominated by newspapers has been replaced by one dominated by television, the British analyst Anthony Smith concludes:

> The newspaper-dominated system emphasized the continuity of voters' political affiliations. The audience was divided into partisan groupings, each of whom received information from the parties themselves and from the printed media organizationally connected with them or supporting them as a matter of editorial policy. Party loyalty entailed newspaper loyalty and normally also membership in a defined social and economic group. The strength of these identifications in turn reinforced the stability of the party system. But television works differently on all of these scores. Because it aspires to impartiality and because its audience is less differentiated, less often self-selected, than the readership of the political press, television exposes more of the people more of the time to views different from those they already hold. By showing both sides of an argument, it tends to erode the stability of people's political views and party identification and even the stability of the party system. It has this effect all the more where it gives equal time to all parties, encouraging new factions to fight elections.[43]

Kurt and Gladys Lang report that in August 1952, some weeks after the television networks had for the first time provided extensive coverage of the national party conventions, the Radio Corporation of America (which owns NBC) ran a full-page advertisement in the *New York Times* proclaiming:

> With the aid of television, we had what amounted to the biggest town meeting ever held . . . 60 million people had front-row seats

Television's Impact on American Politicians

and got a better picture of what was going on than any delegate or any reporter on the convention floor.... Because of television, American citizens will be better informed than they ever were before.... They will be able to vote for men and principles, and not for party labels.[44]

All three networks could make the same claim in the 1980s with even greater force—and there is no reason to suppose that they have changed their view that their portrayal of politics is helping to make a more informed public and a more truly democratic America—and if that has the side effects of displacing and weakening the parties, so what?

How Politicians Use Television

At the beginning of this chapter we noted John Sears's view that, while politicians playing the political game might be happier with some rules and playing conditions than others, their job is to try to turn to their own advantage whatever rules and conditions set for them. Thus we may be sure that American politicians are well aware that how they and their issues and personalities come across on television is crucial to their success or failure. Constantly popping up in their discussions of strategy and tactics are such questions as: How can we get the kind of television exposure we want? How can we keep the networks from making us look bad? This is obvious in their campaigning operations, but it is also true in their policy-making activities, as we shall see.

IN CAMPAIGNS

We noted earlier that one of the prime objectives of every campaign for a public office with a large constituency is to get as much free and favorable exposure as possible on local and national newscasts and interview shows that are likely to be seen by the constituency's voters. Television news producers know very well that all manner of candidates are constantly trying to get such exposure, and they are wary of the possibility that their shows might serve a candidate's purposes more than the broadcasters'. Hence if they are convinced that a particular campaign event is a pure "mediality," manufactured out of whole cloth by some media consultant for free air time, they are likely to ignore it—unless, of course, it is just too audience-grabbing to pass up.

Accordingly, one of the most valued tricks of the consultant's trade is knowing how to invent and stage campaign events that will serve *both* the broadcasters' needs for good visuals and newsworthiness *and* the candidate's need for free and favorable exposure. To that end the best consultants have come up with a variety of imaginative gimmicks. One of the most familiar is described by Larry Sabato:

> The "walking" candidate is a favorite. More than a quarter century ago an obscure Nevada journalist, Thomas Mechling, trekked across his state to upset the favored candidate for a Democratic U.S. Senate nomination. Trudging across a constituency became a successful tactic again in the early 1970s. First "walkin' Lawton" Chiles plodded his way 1,003 miles down the Florida peninsula to win a Senate seat in 1970. Then Dan Walker (appropriately named) became governor of Illinois, and Dick Clark upset an incumbent U.S. senator in Iowa in 1972 using the technique. After that the dam broke, and literally hundreds of candidates have, with varying degrees of success, joined the fad and put on their walking boots.[45]

Another imaginative and successful gimmick was the "work day" approach invented by media consultant Robert Squier for an obscure Florida state senator, Bob Graham, in his campaign for the 1978 Democratic gubernatorial nomination. Squier arranged for Graham to work one day each at 100 mainly blue-collar jobs. During his lunch hour on the tenth

Television's Impact on American Politicians

day Graham called a press conference, announced his candidacy, and said his work days were intended to help him learn the real problems, thoughts, and feelings of the people of Florida. For each of the remaining ninety days he was followed by a number of reporters and often appeared on television newscasts. Squier also had his own cameras at the scenes, and in the paid advertisements he produced later he used film clips of Graham teaching a class while Graham's voice-over discussed his educational policies, clips of Graham driving a truck while Graham was giving his views on transportation policy, and so on. It worked splendidly: Graham began as an unknown, but he finished second in the first round of the primary with 25 percent of the votes in a field of seven. He then won the runoff primary with 53 percent and the general election with 55 percent.[46]

This has its social costs, of course, not the least of which is a certain trivialization of the campaigns. Thomas Patterson's study of media coverage of the 1976 presidential election campaign found that nearly three-fifths of the networks' coverage dealt with the "horse race" aspects (who was gaining or losing, how campaign strategies were changing, the size of crowds at airport rallies and motorcades) and less than a third on substance (the candidates' stands on the issues and their records in prior offices). This was a higher proportion of trivia than in any of the newspapers and news magazines, but not much higher.[47]

Even the participants are sometimes put off by the televisation of everything. For example, Malcolm MacDougall, the staff director of advertising for Gerald Ford's campaign in 1976, reported television's campaign coverage as he saw it on his own set:

> I saw Carter playing softball in Plains, Georgia. I saw Carter kissing Amy, I saw Carter hugging Lillian. I saw Carter, in dungarees, walking hand in hand through the peanut farm with Rosalynn. I saw Carter going into church, preaching in church, coming out of

church. I saw Carter trying to explain his ethnic purity statement. I saw Carter trying to explain his *Playboy* interview. And then I saw two full, wonderful weeks of people commenting about Carter's *Playboy* interview. I saw Ford misstate the problems of Eastern Europe—and a week of people commenting about his misstatement. I saw Ford bump his head again. I saw Ford in Ohio say how glad he was to be back in Iowa. I saw marching bands and hecklers, and I learned about the size of crowds and the significance of the size of the crowds. And I saw Carter carrying his own suitcase a lot. But in all the hours of high anxiety that I spent watching the network news, never did I hear what the candidates had to say about the campaign issues. That was not news.[48]

And even the successful candidate was not delighted with the coverage. A year later Jimmy Carter told a reporter:

> It's a strange thing that you can go through your campaign for president, and you have a basic theme that you express in a 15— or 20-minute standard speech that you give over and over and over; and the traveling press—sometimes exceeding 100 people— will never report that speech to the public. The peripheral aspects become the headlines, but the basic essence of what you stand for and what you hope to accomplish is never reported.[49]

Nevertheless, the networks and the press have their own needs and their own ideas of how best to serve them. Hence any campaign organization that depends on free television exposure as well as on paid advertisements has no choice but to accommodate to their schedules and try to provide material the networks will find worth broadcasting. And that is what they do no matter how they may deplore the resulting trivialization of the campaign.

IN GOVERNMENT

Direct Publicity. Politicians' efforts to use the great power of television and the other mass media for their own ends do not, of course, cease between elections. Indeed, just about ev-

Television's Impact on American Politicians

ery government agency and high official, elected or appointed, understands perfectly well that what the public thinks the politicians are doing in formulating and executing public policy comes in part from what the newspapers say but mostly from what television shows.

Accordingly, they are all conscious, as they must be, of the need to have the best possible "public relations" if they are to get the legislation, appropriations, and appointments they want. So each executive department and administrative agency has an office for public relations, usually well staffed and constantly busy. For instance, a sampling of the major executive agencies in 1982 shows an Office of Public Affairs in the Department of Defense, an Office of Public Information in the Department of Labor, a Bureau of Public Affairs in the Department of State, and an Office of Communications in the Executive Office of the President. Moreover, most of the major subdivisions of the departments have their own public relations offices, and the same is true of the independent regulatory commissions: for example, the Environmental Protection Agency has both an Office of Public Awareness and an Office of Press Services, the Federal Communications Commission has an Office of Public Affairs, the Federal Trade Commission has an Office of Public Information, and so on.[50]

Much the same is true of members of Congress. Michael Robinson reports that in 1960 there were very few persons called "press secretaries" on senators' staffs and almost none on representatives' staffs; but in 1980, 97 senators listed at least one press aide and many listed two or three, while over 200 members of the House listed at least one. Moreover, in 1980 the Senate had three and the House had six recording studios in which the members could tape radio or video messages for their constituents at costs far below what commercial studios would charge, and over 80 percent of the members used these services.

Since 1979, the House has regularly provided live video

117

coverage of its floor proceedings, broadcast by over 850 cable television stations across the nation on C-Span (Cable-Satellite Public Affairs Network). The national broadcasting networks use only a few clips of the House proceedings every now and then, in part because they object to the House leadership's decision to retain exclusive control of the coverage: the House's technicians operate the cameras, the cameras are kept fixed on the podium and the well, and so there are no shots, comparable to those the networks feature so lavishly in their broadcasts of the national party conventions, of members napping, reading newspapers, or otherwise appearing unstatesmanlike.[51]

It is important to remember, in this regard, that a good deal of the material the networks as well as the newspapers use for their stories on what the various agencies of government are doing is taken from the handouts produced in great profusion by all these executive, legislative, and administrative public relations offices. The handouts are particularly important for television news. The expense of maintaining a lot of camera crews and moving them frequently from one spot to another is so great that the broadcasters much prefer to cover officially scheduled events (press conferences, committee hearings, prearranged interviews, and the like) that will provide them with plenty of pictures of good technical quality at a reasonable cost. The network news divisions are not geared up for a lot of investigative reporting of their own, and so they depend mainly on newspapers, wire services, and official handouts for most of their information about what is going on and what is worth filming.[52] But official handouts are by no means the only method public officials use for getting their messages to the media.

"Leaks". One of the most important and least studied media techniques used by public officials to achieve their policy objectives is the "leak," by which I mean the secret and unauthorized transmission of confidential material by a public offi-

Television's Impact on American Politicians

cial to a media outlet for publication or broadcasting. There is as yet no comprehensive study of leaks,[53] but it is clear that they go back a long way in American history and that they have increased in number and impact since the end of World War II. There are many examples of leaks in recent years; among the best known are the following:

In 1968, the Department of Defense prepared a 7,000-page secret study of how the United States had become involved in the Vietnam War. In 1971, the study was photocopied and leaked to the *New York Times* by Daniel Ellsberg, a former special assistant in the office of International Security Affairs, who hoped that publishing the documents would discredit the war and force the government to end it.[54] A government suit resulted in a Supreme Court decision upholding the newspaper's right to publish such materials over the protests of the president and the Department of Defense.

A more recent example was the publication by the *Washington Post* in February 1982 of an account of several confidential meetings of Secretary of State Alexander M. Haig, Jr. with his top aides. The *Post* said that the story was based on "notes taken by one of the people present at nearly two dozen regular senior staff meetings over the last year." It reported Haig as saying, among other things, that the British foreign secretary, Lord Carrington, was a "duplicitous bastard," that the Camp David accords were bound to fall apart, and that the Saudi Arabians "have an arrogant mentality that is absolutely devastating."[55] The State Department's Bureau of Security immediately launched an investigation to discover the leaker's identity, but none was reported and Haig's resignation in June 1982 made the question moot.

Another recent example came in January 1982 when the *Washington Post* published a report of a secret Defense Department study concluding that the Reagan administration's five-year rearmament program would cost $750 billion more than publicly announced. The administration was furious, and lie detector tests were required for all persons who had attended the meeting at which the study was reported. On the basis of these tests, John Tillson, the department's manpower management director, was dismissed. The *Post's* reporter who had written the story denied that Tillson had leaked the information to him, but Tillson's dismissal stuck nevertheless.[56]

Every president, at least since Harry Truman, has complained about leaks. Truman lamented, "Ninety-five percent of our secret information has been revealed in newspapers and slick magazines and that's what I am trying to stop." Lyndon Johnson repeatedly told his aides, "This goddamn town leaks like a wornout boot." Gerald Ford declared, "I'm damned sick and tired of a ship that has such leaky seams. We are being drowned by premature and obvious leaks." Jimmy Carter told State Department officials that "if there was another outbreak of misinformation, distortions, or self-serving leaks, I would direct the Secretary of State to discharge the officials responsible for that particular desk, even if some innocent people might be punished." Ronald Reagan exploded that he was "up to his keister" in leaks from his subordinates. And Richard Nixon went furthest of all. After learning of Ellsberg's disclosure of the Pentagon papers, he told his staff:

> I don't give a damn how it is done, do whatever has to be done to stop these leaks and prevent further unauthorized disclosures; I don't want to be told why it can't be done. This government cannot survive, it cannot function, if anyone can run out and leak whatever documents he wants to. . . . I want to know who is behind this and I want the most complete investigation that can be conducted. . . . I don't want excuses. I want results. I want it done, whatever the cost.[57]

He was as good as his word. His aides met his demands by forming the subsequently notorious "plumbers' unit" to plug the leaks. Some of their tactics, such as tapping various sus-

Television's Impact on American Politicians

pected leakers' telephones and burglarizing the offices of Ellsberg's psychiatrist, became part of what are known as "the Watergate horrors."

For our purposes, however, the point to note is that leaks are here to stay, and for a very good reason: both the leakers and the news media have a good deal to gain from them.

The leakers often find them to be the best way of gaining one or more of several different objectives. For one, they may wish to float a "trial balloon" about a contemplated policy so that they can see, before it is presented as a firm policy commitment, what kinds of reactions it evokes from the media, the public, and other public officials. For another, they may wish to get other officials and agencies to back off from adopting policies the leakers disapprove. For still another, the leakers may wish to discredit other public officials and/or make themselves look good. And most useful of all, leaks give public officials a kind of control over what the media report and emphasize that they can get no other way: after all, if they are headlining information you have given them, they can't be embarrassing you with information they have dug up elsewhere.

The news media also find leaks very useful. They provide in the easiest possible way information the media could otherwise not get at all or get only with great effort and expense. Leaks are often made exclusively to particular reporters or broadcast correspondents, thereby providing the scoops that are valued so highly in news business competition. Leaks also provide heretofore secret information, which gives the resulting stories an air of excitement, of going behind the scenes, of revealing what is *really* going on, that is usually absent from stories based on official handouts. So it is not surprising that the media are glad to receive leaks whenever and wherever they can.

Conclusion

In chapter 2 a good deal was made of the adversary posture television's newspeople characteristically take toward politics and politicians. In this chapter we have seen that there is also something of a symbiotic relationship between the news media and the politicians. The producers of television news certainly use the politicians as rich material for shows that will achieve their prime purpose of attracting and keeping the largest possible audiences, and the byproducts of the way they characteristically portray politicians have done a good deal of damage to the general repute and operating strength of political parties and politicians.

Yet the media-politician relationship works the other way as well. Politicians, in public office or out, have no doubt that, like it or not, they have to operate in a world in which political reality for most people is what television says it is. They are well aware of television's great power not only to make life difficult for them but also to enable them to bring their messages and personalities to far more people far more effectively than they can by any other means. So they do their best, often with success, to use both paid and free television exposure for their own ends.

In short, television and politicians are in a symbiotic as well as an adversarial relationship because they need each other. Their relationship is always uneasy and often quarrelsome, but it is permanent. And it sets many of the most important circumstances within which governing in America must be conducted. In chapter 5 we shall consider how the advent of television has affected those circumstances.

Chapter 5

Governing in the Television Age

FOR MOST political scientists the last and most important question about any change in the circumstances of our polity is: What are its effects upon the way we govern ourselves? That is, how does it affect the processes by which our governments choose and carry out their public policies? How does it affect the kinds of policies they choose and reject?

Many observers, including myself, believe that the advent of television is the most important change since World War II in just about every aspect of American life, and certainly in the environment in which government functions. In the preceding chapters we have reviewed television's role as the dominant portrayer of political reality for most Americans, the manner in which it depicts politics, its impact on how our politicians go about their business.

In this chapter we come to the political scientist's core question: How has television affected the way America is governed? As with so many matters considered in this book, my answers to that question can only be reasonable explanations, educated guesses, and my best judgments, not scientifically precise and final truths. Nor can I say with confidence or credibility that in any particular instance television is the sole or even the most powerful cause of the effects in question. For television, like everything else in our complex society, operates in, affects, and is affected by a great web of other social forces and institutions. In most cases the tools of political science are too crude to isolate the influence of television from all other influences. It is, therefore, impossible to determine precisely and accurately just how much of any particular change in our ways of governing is caused by television alone.

Even so, the questions are too important to suspend all judgments until we can provide perfect answers. So let us tackle them now as best we can.

Television's Compression of Time

It seems to me that one of television's most obvious and important effects is that it has significantly compressed the time American governments have in which to institute programs and achieve the results needed to sustain those programs as long as may be necessary for politicians, and the rest of us, to get their full benefit.

We should recognize at the start that at least two elements of our governing system, fixed terms of office and short intervals between elections, have always put more pressure for quick results on American administrations than on their counterparts in the parliamentary democracies.

For example, Margaret Thatcher became Great Britain's prime minister on May 4, 1979 and Ronald Reagan became president of the United States on January 20, 1981. The two leaders offered similar, though not identical, new programs to

Governing in the Television Age

cure their countries' economic ills: both aimed to end inflation and promote economic growth by measures liberating business from excessive government regulation, cutting taxes and expenditures, and holding down the supply of money and credit.

There was, however, at least one significant difference between their situations. Under the British system no general election had to be held for five years, although, like any prime minister, Mrs. Thatcher could have called one at any time she wished before the five years had elapsed. Moreover, her Conservative party held seventy more seats in the House of Commons than Labour, the chief opposition party, and forty-three more seats than all the other parties combined. Accordingly, so long as her party stood solidly behind her (as British governing parties almost always do), she had a full five years in which to put her radical new economic program in place and have it produce the results—reduced inflation, increased growth, a stronger currency, and eventually lower unemployment—that would prove it a success and win her and her party another term in office.

Ronald Reagan, on the other hand, took office knowing that an election for all the members of the House of Representatives and one-third of the members of the Senate would take place on November 2, 1982 whether it was convenient for him or not. That meant that he, like any new American president, had, not five years, but a little over twenty-one months in which to put his program in place (which was especially difficult since the opposition Democrats controlled a majority of the seats in the House of Representatives) and show the results that would convince the voters the program was working and thereby persuade them to vote for his fellow Republicans in the congressional elections.

When Margaret Thatcher's first twenty-one months in office had expired, her economic program was doing very poorly: in January 1981 unemployment had risen sharply, business failures had risen almost as sharply, inflation had declined very little, interest rates continued high, the pound sterling was weaker than ever against other currencies, and the public opinion polls showed that if she had had to face an election at that time the Conservatives would have been badly beaten. But she did not have to face an election then, and her successful conduct of the 1982 mini-war with Argentina over the Falkland Islands restored her popularity and made her reelection prospects look much better. And she still had over three years in which her economic program could show favorable results before she had to call for the next general election. She eventually called the election for June 9, 1983, and her Conservatives won an even larger parliamentary majority.

By contrast, when Ronald Reagan's first twenty-one months were up, his economic program seemed to be doing somewhat better than Mrs. Thatcher's: despite the Democrats' control of the House, he got Congress to make major cuts in spending on domestic programs; inflation fell sharply, interest rates inched down, and the dollar grew much stronger against other currencies. On the other hand, unemployment rose to record postwar levels, business failures rose sharply, and he had no Falklands-style triumph in foreign affairs to offset his domestic economic difficulties. So in the 1982 elections the Republicans lost a net of twenty-six seats in the House of Representatives and barely managed to hold their own in the Senate despite the fact that nearly twice as many Democratic as Republican seats were risk.

For whatever consolation it may have been, the short intervals between elections resulted in Ronald Reagan doing no worse than any of his predecessors except one. With the single exception of Franklin D. Roosevelt and the Democrats in 1934, the party of every president since the Civil War has lost seats in the House of Representatives in the midterm election of his first term.[1] So it seems that the American institutions of fixed terms of office and short intervals between elections[2] provide

Governing in the Television Age

every American president, Republican or Democrat, conservative or liberal, with every little time to put his program in place and get the kind of results he needs for his party to do well in the first election it must face after he takes office.

These institutional constraints, of course, handicapped American presidents and their parties for nearly two centuries before the advent of television. But I believe that the way television has presented politics since the 1950s has compressed even more the time elected officials and administrations have to install programs and get results.

For one thing, entertainment television is full of dramas and "docudramas" in which a problem of some sort, often social or political, is set forth, fought through, and resolved in an hour or two, minus commercials. One result is surely a spreading of the general assumption that life's problems can be understood and resolved quickly, with no messy strings left dangling, if only people with vision and courage deal with them. And in political campaigns that assumption is reinforced by the floods of political advertisements and stories on the nightly news in which challengers attack incumbents for their failure to produce all the good things they promised and proclaim that "it's time for a change" in the people running things if the nation is to get what it wants. Judged in the light of such expectations, inflated as they are by television's presentation of life and candidates' presentations of their opponents, real-life results are likely to seem disappointing at best and often downright disgraceful.

For another thing, television, as we saw in chapter 2, has an insatiable appetite for news stories, especially stories that are pictorially interesting, dramatic, up-to-the-minute, based on "hard facts," and new. It also has a strong penchant for "horse race" journalism. These two drives combine to make newscasters avid for all kinds of political "scores"—that is, news items that, like sports scores, are expressed in numbers, go up or down, and change often enough to keep providing new stories. This leads the newscasters to pay a lot of attention to election matters. They find a real bonanza in a presidential year, with its many polls on the candidates' standings, its dozens of presidential primaries, its convention balloting, and election night in November, "the Superbowl of the news divisions." It also leads the newscasters to feature a kind of perpetual temperature-taking that focuses on short-term and often minor ups and downs in the state of the union.

One classic illustration of this is the newscasters' use of economic indicators.[3] Every month various agencies of the federal government issue a total of between forty and fifty reports on the current readings of various economic indexes. Some of the most familiar include the size of the gross national product, the rate of economic growth (or decline), the consumer price index, prices paid to farmers for raw agricultural products, the percentage of the work force unemployed, the country's international balance of payments, consumer installment debt, average personal income, housing starts, a general index of leading economic indicators, and the arcane "M-1" (the basic money supply of currency in circulation and in checking account deposits). And five days a week the Dow Jones company reports its famous composite index of the price of leading industrial stocks.

The network newscasters usually "annualize" each month's figure: for example, if February's consumer price index is up .7 percent over January's, the "annual inflation rate" is reported to be running at 8.4 percent (.7 × 12 = 8.4) on a twelve-months basis.

Annualized thus, these monthly indexes are ideal items for the networks' stories on the state of the economy. Since they come from official government reports, they are hard news, and they are easily presented in eye-catching color graphics, sometimes with animated trend lines marching up or down. They permit, even demand, frequent reports from many different angles on the how-the-economy-is-doing theme, and, perhaps most important of all, they are expressed in numbers, they come out every month, there are a lot of them, and they are reported on different days. In fact they serve the news divisions' purposes almost as well as sports scores serve the sports divisions' purposes. So the networks' newscasters report them, regularly and with emphasis.

Some present and former government economists doubt that paying so much attention to these indexes is in the public interest. For example, as Herbert Stein, professor of economics at the University of Virginia and chairman of the Council of Economic Advisors under President Nixon, reported from his own experience in office:

> I felt constantly harassed by the reporting of the economic statistics in the press and on TV, which seems to me to always be making a big deal out of each month's figures. Each month's figures, of course, seemed to be worse than the previous month's, and each month's figures were made to seem much more . . . record-setting and historical than they really deserved to be. There seemed to be very little possibility of getting a big picture out of the daily reporting. . . . I felt that this was more than an irritation to me, that it did have some adverse effects on life in this country, that it kept the public in a constant state of anxiety and nervousness about the economy. The fact that our economy was producing the highest standard of living any community had ever enjoyed . . . was being lost in a kind of hypochondria about each month's statistics.

Stein particularly objected to the "annualization" of the up and down twitches of each monthly index figure, but George Herman, a leading economics correspondent for CBS News, replied:

> When it comes to price indexes, the question then arises as a communicator, . . . which does the great American public out there sitting in front of their television sets with a can of beer or a nice martini in one hand and spanking a child with the other hand, which do they understand better, that prices went up four-tenths of one percent or that they were going up at a rate of, say five

percent a year.... When we are in our car driving along and we look down at the dashboard, we don't want to know that we went three-tenths of a mile in the last minute. We want to know how many miles an hour we're doing.

Stein was not convinced. He replied:

> The point is whether you are reporting the actual state of the economy or whether you are reporting some fluff which gives an unrealistic picture of the vacillations of the economy and therefore creates unrealistic and undeserved jitters.... When the [Washington] Bullets win a basketball game, you don't say ... the Bullets played last night at a rate which, if continued through the season, would give them the [championship]. That's just one game. And you don't report every game ... the same as you would report the playoffs.[4]

Presidents Ford and Carter and their economic advisors made similar complaints about the networks' reporting of economic news, and in March 1982 President Reagan complained in a newspaper interview that:

> You can't turn on the evening news without seeing that they're going to interview someone else who has lost his job or they're outside the factory that has laid off workers or so forth—the constant downbeat—that can contribute to slowing down a new recovery that is in the offing.... Television is an entertainment medium ... looking for the eye-catching and spectacular, but is it news that some fellow out in South Succotash someplace has just been laid off that he should be interviewed nationwide?[5]

Before and since the president's criticism, however, the networks have continued to report and annualize each month's leading economic indexes and to illustrate some of the more dramatic results with "human interest" examples of the sort that annoyed President Reagan (himself a former television professional). And presidents and their economic advisors have continued to believe that such reporting spreads the idea that their administrations have the power not only to manage

Governing in the Television Age

the economy but even to fine-tune it. By drawing the audiences' attention to the short-term "scores" of the annualized monthly index reports, they believe, the networks make it far more difficult for an administration to show the kind of results they need to sustain any program long enough to deal effectively with the economy's basic problems. But then it should surprise no reader of this book to learn that making it easier for administrations to sustain long-range economic programs does not, to say the least, rank high among the criteria by which the network newscasters decide what news they will report and how they will present it. Television's world moves fast, its events are dramatic, and things are always changing rapidly. Like it or not, that is the world in which presidents, economic advisors, and administrations of either party must live as best they can.

Reducing Options

In chapter 4 we considered the phenomenon of leaks, the process by which policy makers secretly use the news media to promote policies or persons they favor, and the media use the policy-makers' revelations to get, with little effort, inside information they otherwise could only get with difficulty or not at all. Leaks are effective ways in which both the government side and the media side of a usually adversarial relationship can use the other side's special position to promote its own interests. Its main effect on the governing process, however, is often to spotlight, always prematurely and sometimes unwisely, possible policy options in a way that eliminates them from further serious consideration. Two prominent recent examples illustrate this point. One is provided by what happened in 1982 to a policy option of taxing unemployment benefits being considered by the Reagan administration. One of the many tough problems created for the administration by the severe economic recession of 1982 was the dilemma posed by the rising deficits in the federal budget. As more and more businesses failed and unemployment rose from 6 percent when Reagan took office to over 10 percent in the Autumn of 1982, revenues from taxes on business earnings and personal incomes declined. At the same time the government's outlays for unemployment compensation rose sharply. The combination of falling revenues and rising costs increased the federal deficit from an estimated $80 to $90 billion at the beginning of the year to an estimated $150 billion or more by November. Such a huge deficit not only shattered the traditional and cherished image of Republicans as budget balancers but also forced much greater government borrowing to meet its obligations; and this, in turn, put great new pressure on the credit markets, helped to keep interest rates up, and posed a real danger for the administration's success in lowering the rate of inflation.

Clearly something, probably a lot of things, had to be done about the soaring deficits, and done as soon as possible. But what? The administration's economic advisors were of several different minds and they offered a variety of options. In late November a front-page story in the *Washington Post* reported that a sixteen-page paper had been sent to the president by the Cabinet Council on Economic Affairs setting forth a number of options for dealing with the deficit and with high and rising unemployment. One of the options, the story said, was "a proposal to tax the benefits paid to those out of work."[6]

All the national news media, especially the network newscasters, immediately made this leak their top story. The next day they asked the White House deputy press secretary, Larry Speakes, to confirm or deny the report. Speakes replied that such a tax was indeed one of many options currently under consideration, and the underlying idea of it would be to remove one of the attractions of unemployment benefits and

Governing in the Television Age

thereby provide an incentive for people to look harder for jobs and get off unemployment compensation. If it worked, Speakes said, it would reduce unemployment, increase tax revenues, and help reduce the deficit.

His statements were featured by all the networks that night, and all of them, in their accustomed manner of complying with the Federal Communication Act's fairness doctrine (see chapter 2), broadcast angry rebuttal statements by labor leaders and Democrats to the effect that imposing such a penalty on the millions of newly-unemployed, who were far from being "welfare bums," would constitute an attack on their moral character as well as an additional blow to their financial condition.

A few days later Speakes announced that the proposal, which, he reminded the reporters, had only been one of a number of options put before the president, had been dropped from further consideration.

I am not concerned here with whether the proposal was a good idea or a poor one. My point is that the network coverage and the consequent protests forced the idea to be dropped before the administration had had time to consider thoroughly its likely economic and political costs and benefits. Strictly speaking, it was the administration which made the decision to abandon the option, but in fact the glare of television's lights and cameras had forced the administration's hand, and they now had one less option to consider than they would have preferred at this early stage.

An even more vivid example is provided by the impact of television's coverage on an administration's ability to fight wars with limited objectives, that is, where less than our country's very survival is at stake. Many observers believe, for example, that television's coverage of the Vietnam War played a central role in our ultimate withdrawal and defeat. Certainly Lyndon Johnson thought so. We noted in chapter 1 that his decision to wind down the war and to forego a second elective term in office was precipitated by Walter Cronkite's famous broadcast declaring the war a failure. The day after he had announced his decision not to seek another term, Johnson said, in a speech to an especially appropriate audience, the National Association of Broadcasters:

> As I sat in my office last evening, waiting to speak, I thought of the many times each week when television brings the war into the American home. No one can say exactly what effect those vivid scenes would have on American opinion. Historians must only guess at the effect that television would have had during earlier conflicts on the future of this Nation: during the Korean war, for example, at that time when our forces were pushed back there to Pusan; or World War II, the Battle of the Bulge, or when our men were slugging it out in Europe or when most of our Air Force was shot down that day in June off Australia.[7]

Some analysts have agreed with Johnson that television played a crucial role. They contend that the networks featured night after night on-the-spot films in vivid color showing American troops killing, being killed, and even committing atrocities, such as putting cigarette lighter flames to the poor thatched huts of Vietnamese peasants; and they portrayed the Vietcong's "Tet" offensive of 1968 as a great defeat rather than the considerable military victory it was for American arms. The effect of their coverage was to convince Americans that the war was immoral, or that, immoral or not, we were losing it. The end result, they believe, was to create a climate of public opinion in which it was impossible to win the war or even continue it.[8]

Whatever may be the merits of this argument, it is interesting to note that in 1982 the British government of Margaret Thatcher, facing a limited-objective war with Argentina in the Falkland Islands, prohibited on-the-spot filming of the action by the BBC and other British television news services. As an American reporter wrote from London:

Governing in the Television Age

Television networks were prevented from broadcasting live from the Royal Navy's Falklands task force, and their film of events in the South Atlantic took weeks to reach London by ship and plane. So the war was nearly over before Britons saw dramatic scenes of the destruction of some of their warships or heard emotional interviews with survivors. Still photographs of burning British warships, transmitted more quickly to London, were blocked from publication by military censors for days and sometimes weeks.

Mrs. Thatcher and her cabinet colleagues stated quite frankly that night-after-night televising of pictures of the inevitable destruction and bloodshed would make it much more difficult for her government to do what had to be done to drive the Argentine invaders off the islands. And Sir Frank Cooper, the top civil servant in the Defense Ministry, acknowledged that in their official statements about the progress of the war, "We aimed throughout not to lie; but there were occasions when we did not tell the whole truth and did not correct things that were being misread."[9]

The BBC and the commercial television network complained bitterly, but they were confined to showing stock prewar footage of the area and a few films from Argentine sources and to putting their own commentators' "talking heads" before the cameras speculating about what was really going on in the South Atlantic. This, in turn, made the government complain about television's critical and unhelpful (some said downright unpatriotic) coverage of the war.

But Mrs. Thatcher's government had an option effectively denied to Lyndon Johnson or any American president. Great Britain has no written constitution, no formal protection of freedom of the press comparable to that in the American First Amendment, and no Supreme Court with the power to declare unconstitutional acts approved, as Mrs. Thatcher's were, by a majority of the House of Commons. The United States has all of these, and it also has a television industry that uses them for all they are worth. The industry also believes that its proper function is, not to make things easier for presidents and administrations to carry out their limited wars or any other policies, but to make sure that their viewers are fully aware of what those policies really are and how well or badly they are really working. It therefore seems unlikely that any future American administration can sustain very long, or perhaps even seriously consider launching, a war fought on foreign soil for objectives more limited than our country's survival.

Some would argue that that is a very good thing, for it will prevent us from ever again sinking into bloody quagmires like Korea or Vietnam. Others would say it is a bad thing, for it deprives us of an option often used by our Soviet adversaries and their allies, and leaves us with no serious military option except total nuclear war.[10] Whatever may be the right evaluation, however, television's effective elimination of the limited-war option seems undeniable, and that in itself will make the conduct of foreign policy significantly different in the age of television than it was in the 1960s and before.

Weakening the Coalition Builders

THE PROBLEM: A GOVERNMENT OF CONFLICTING PARTS

Whenever one considers what is happening to the American system of governance, it is well to remember that that system was designed in 1787 by fifty-five men who recognized the necessity of a strong government but feared that such a government might become too strong and that its power might be captured by a single faction or interest bent on advancing its position at the expense of all others. They believed that it is better for government not to act at all than for it to act over the strong objections of any significant part of the community.

Governing in the Television Age

They certainly had no intention of maximizing in America the kind of teamwork that has become characteristic of most other Western democracies today, in which government is conducted by one team of politicians in power while its policies and actions are opposed by a team that stands ready to take power when the voters decide it is time to change policies and leaders.

The men of 1787 built many well-conceived and effective devices into the formal constitutional system to achieve their goals. They divided the total power of government between the states and the national government. They divided the national government's power among its three branches and they prohibited any person from serving in more than one branch at a time. They provided that the persons occupying the leading offices in each branch would serve for terms of different lengths, be selected by different constituencies, and be chosen at sufficiently different intervals that there would never be a British-style "general election" in which all the officeholders could be swept out of office on a wave of strong though temporary popular passion. And they crowned the system with an elaborate set of checks and balances to ensure that each branch could delay or prevent action by the other branches.

All this is familiar enough, and almost as familiar is the fact that the formal constitutional system is strongly reinforced by many aspects of our political culture. One aspect of that culture is our continuing dislike of government, or any other political or social organization, that grows too large and powerful. Public opinion polls today show that most Americans continue to dislike big government, big business, and big labor with equal intensity. Another aspect is our low opinion of political parties and partisanship, which we discussed in chapter 3. Still another is our perennial admiration of "independent" officeholders who stand proudly free from "dictation" by the "party bosses," and the "independent" voter whose eyes are unclouded by party labels and who votes for the best candidate for each office.[11]

TRADITIONAL SOLUTIONS

The traditional American constitutional system and political culture has well satisfied the nation's needs for keeping government and politicians from damaging our liberties very much for very long. But our country, like all countries, has from time to time needed a government able to take strong and concerted action in a crisis, such as a war or a major depression, when we cannot afford either inaction or action that goes off in conflicting directions. In such situations we have had to face a basic if unpalatable fact of life.

For testimony on this point I turn to an improbable witness from a time that seems very remote from the 1980s: During the height of the "flower children" Eden in San Francisco's Haight-Ashbury district in the 1960s, a group calling themselves "the diggers" came every day to Golden Gate Park to distribute free food to all who asked for it. An observer who had studied the movement in its heyday returned in the early 1970s and found that the free food was no longer available. He searched out one of the few remaining members of the movement and asked him why. The veteran "digger" replied:

> Well, man, it took a lot of organization to get that done. We had to scuffle to get the food. Then the chicks or somebody had to prepare it. Then we got to serve it. A lot of people got to do a lot of things at the right time or it doesn't come off. Well, it got so that people weren't doing it. I mean a cat wouldn't let us have his truck when we needed it or some chick is grooving somewhere and can't help out. Now you hate to get into a power bag and start telling people what to do, but without that, man, well . . .[12]

In whatever idiom we may speak, Americans have learned that there are times when our government must get something

Governing in the Television Age

done, and on those occasions a lot of people have got to do a lot of things at the right time or it doesn't come off. There are times that demand organization, coordination, and direction in government, and when those times come the nation needs some agencies that can make working coalitions out of the fragmented and independent individuals, groups, and institutions at hand. In our two centuries of existence under our present constitutional system we have developed several agencies for building such coalitions. And in the age of television, most have been significantly weakened.

Strong Presidents. Whatever may have been the Founding Fathers' intentions for the presidency, the fact is that since the time of Andrew Jackson (1829–1837) the nation has depended heavily upon vigorous leadership by its presidents, especially in times of special need for strong and concerted action, to gather together enough of the scattered fragments of power to enable the government to steer a set course rather than drift about in its normal aimless fashion. Indeed, the office has become so central to our version of democracy that we have come to call it "presidential democracy" rather than "separational" or "divided" democracy. Most analysts would now agree that most of the time, and especially in times of crisis, the government works well when the presidency is working well and badly when it is not.[13]

Television has had strong but mixed effects on the presidency. On the one hand, it has given considerably more attention to the presidency than to Congress or any other agency of the national government: All three networks today have four full-time White House correspondents and only two congressional correspondents (and even they are not always full-time). This imbalance in coverage has helped to make the presidency the center of American government and politics even more than it was before television. As Michael Schudson explains:

It should not be surprising ... that when television came along, network news departments devoted disproportionate time to covering the presidency. The technology and economics of television make this a likely choice, of course. Since television equipment is expensive and awkward, and can be moved around less easily than the lone reporter with pencil and notepad, film crews tend to be centered in just a few locations, with the result that those locations—especially Washington—gain great emphasis in the TV news. And with the still-current understandings of politics that began decades ago to shift attention from Capitol Hill to the White House, the TV watch on the president was an obvious choice.[14]

Hence the president can command extended segments of prime-time live coverage for his addresses to Congress, his press conferences, his meetings with foreign leaders, his trips abroad, interviews with network correspondents, and a variety of other activities just about any time he pleases. The networks have made presidential nomination and election campaigns the centerpiece of their political coverage, and the presidential campaign debates of 1960, 1976, and 1980 drew vastly greater audiences than those for any other campaign events in our history. Theodore Roosevelt coined a memorable phrase when he called the presidency a "bully pulpit," but television has spotlighted the president and enlarged his congregation far beyond anything T. R. ever knew.

Yet television has in many ways made it harder for a president to succeed than was the case in the first (or, for that matter, the second) Roosevelt's day. By its unblinking stare at what presidential candidates are saying and doing it has not only made them more aware that it is at least as important to look good as to do good, but it has also tempted them to inflate their rhetoric out of all proportion in making their promises, evaluating their achievements, and criticizing their adversaries. The new presidential rhetoric was well exemplified by John F. Kennedy's stirring proclamation in his inaugural address:

Governing in the Television Age

Let every nation know, whether it wishes us well or ill, that we shall pay any price, bear any burden, meet any hardship, support an friend, oppose any foe to assure the survival and the success of liberty.

Television certainly encourages such grandiloquence, and it is bound to inflate people's expectations about what presidents can and should do. If a real-life president were, by some miracle, actually to meet these expectations, television might well put him on some electronic version of Mount Rushmore even before he left office. But there is precious little chance of that. In the television age not only has no president come close to meeting the inflated expectations, but none has even managed to serve two full terms in office: Kennedy was assassinated; Johnson was driven from office by bitterness over the Vietnam War; Nixon resigned to avoid impeachment; and Ford and Carter became, respectively, the first and second incumbents since Herbert Hoover to be defeated for reelection. And, with the exception of Kennedy, the glare of television's coverage had a good deal to do with each president's fall from grace. To see whether Ronald Reagan does better, we shall have to wait a while.

The fact is that the intense television coverage that makes every president's face, voice, and words familiar in just about every American home also, as we have seen, deprives him of some policy options and reduces the time he has to put his programs in place and get the results that will persuade the newscasters to proclaim him a success. And it is worth remembering that no television correspondent or anchorman has ever received an Emmy or a Peabody or even a promotion for a series of broadcasts focusing on what a marvelous job a president (or any other elected official) is doing. Those rewards go to newspeople who expose the moral lapses, lies, and policy failures of public officials, and the president is the biggest game of all in the perennial hunt.

That is how it has been so far in the television age. But what of the future? Political scientist Richard Pious ends his perceptive book on the modern presidency with this comment and prediction:

> Media techniques used during campaigns raise public expectations, whereas subsequent performances of incumbents in office result in a disillusioned and cynical electorate. . . . Interest groups all challenge the president when he attempts to define a national agenda. The media delight in putting incumbents on the defensive, and relish serving up the evidence of double-talk or double-dealing in the executive branch. The legacy of Watergate is wolfpack journalism, which will confirm the worst fears of the public. The White House will remain in a state of siege, as the normal transactions of the political system are unearthed, magnified, and then distorted by the media. Presidential attempts to control the national agenda seemed destined to fail on most issues.[15]

Congress—Closed and Open. In its original "state of nature" as designed by the Founding Fathers, the Congress of the United States is itself one of the most fragmented of the fragments of power that compose the American system of government. It is made up of two equal chambers, and majorities of both must agree on every last word and punctuation mark of every proposed law before it can be sent to the president for his signature or veto. Each member of each house is elected by the voters in a particular part of the nation (a state or a congressional district). Consequently, the first law of political survival for each member is now as it has always been to keep his or her constituents happy. As every member knows, no matter how much the national scorekeepers of the *New York Times*, CBS News, *Human Events*, or the American Political Science Association may admire you, if your constituents come to believe that you are too old to do you job, or too busy being a national figure to keep in touch with the folks back home, or too inept at getting those folks their fair share of the goodies

Governing in the Television Age

handed out by the government, then they are likely to get rid of you at the next election.

Left in its every-member-for-himself "state of nature," the Congress could not possibly pose any threat to the citizens' liberties, for it would be incapable of mounting any kind of collective action for ill or good. But Congress must act collectively and act quite often if the government is to operate at all, let alone operate effectively. From the beginning, accordingly, the members of both houses have developed an elaborate series of formal devices—rules of procedures, committees, legislative calendars, presiding officers, and so on—to coalesce its fragments and undertake some kind of collective action.

Perhaps even more important, in its two centuries of institutional evolution each member has developed an equally elaborate and powerful set of informal understandings, habits, and accepted ways of doing business that have reinforced its formal institutions and made the vital coalition-building process work after a fashion. One such has been the seniority rule, which has provided an easily understood and durable way of filling the leadership posts. Another has been the party organizations (the caucuses, steering committees, and floor leaders) that, while never as strong as their European counterparts, have nevertheless made a major contribution to bringing some order out of the natural chaos. Still another has been such folkways as those requiring that junior members be seen long before they are heard and allowing them to rise in the hierarchy only by proving to their seniors that they have the necessary diligence, reasonableness, and commitment to the rules of the game.[16]

Norman Ornstein has recently pointed out that Congress's long institutional evolution after 1789 culminated in the 1950s in what he calls a "closed system"—that is, a system in which the incentives, rewards, and punishments for congressmen were provided, first, by their constituents and after that by each chamber's own rules and leaders.[17] The mass media, particularly television news, are based mainly in New York and pay far more attention to the president than to Congress as an institution. Except for a few senators who, like Barry Goldwater, Hubert Humphrey, Lyndon Johnson, Estes Kefauver, and John Kennedy, became active candidates for presidential nominations, the media paid even less attention to individual members than to the institution. "All of this meant," says Ornstein, "that legislators could not easily find power, attention, media mentions or celebrity status away from the confines of the Capitol. To a member of Congress, virtually the only way to get ahead was to ride up the power structure inside the house or senate."[18]

Since the political elevators were operated by the senior members and party leaders, the ambitious member had no choice but to conform to the norms of behavior they prescribed. In the often-quoted words of Sam Rayburn, Speaker of the House from 1940 to 1961 and the quintessential closed-system leader, "to get along you have to go along."

Since the 1960s, however, the old ways have changed radically. Congress has become an "open system," and Ornstein makes a convincing case that television has played a major role in that transformation. It began in the 1960s when John Kennedy's success made the Senate a likely place to look for future serious presidential aspirants—and the networks have always been interested in anyone in that category. The Watergate scandals and the impeachment proceedings of 1973–1974 were top stories and brought live national broadcasts of the proceedings of the Ervin committee in the Senate and the Rodino committee in the House.

In addition, the antiestablishment mood generated by the Vietnam War protests, accelerated by Watergate, and sustained by the sharp rise in the volume and prestige of investigative journalism had a major impact on Congress. A wave of reforms in both chambers brought many changes after 1968:

many more subcommittees were created and subcommittee chairmen appointed, and together they weakened the traditional domination of the big parent committees and their chairmen. The staffs of committees, subcommittees, and individual members increased enormously (see below). "Sunshine laws" now require that many once-secret proceedings, such as the committees' "mark-up" sessions in which the details of legislation are worked out, must be open to anyone who cares to attend, including newspaper and television reporters. Many issues that used to be settled by voice votes or teller votes are now settled by roll calls, expedited by the electronic casting and tabulation of the members' votes. Freshmen in both chambers get good committee assignments right from their first days, and the greater number of subcommittees and the higher turnover among the members (see below) advance them much more rapidly than before.

Perhaps most important of all, the networks have discovered that individual congressmen—not only the leaders but also the more colorful and maverick junior members—make for good interviews. So they now appear frequently in the Washington-based interview slots in NBC's "Today," CBS's "Morning News," and ABC's "Good Morning, America" and "Nightline." Ornstein sums up the members' new situation in the 1970s and 1980s thus:

> As media coverage expanded, the number of members of Congress who were brought to public attention mushroomed, and more and more of the publicized members came from the rank and file.... This trend toward personal publicity provided, in contrast to the Rayburn era, a range of tangible and possible outside incentives. No longer did a member have to play by inside rules to receive inside rewards or avoid inside setbacks. One could "go public" and be rewarded by national attention; national attention in turn could provide ego gratification, social success in Washington, the opportunity to run for higher office, or, by highlighting an issue, policy success.[19]

And the folks back home seemed to like it too.

Ornstein concludes that the new "open" Congress performs its part in governing quite differently from the way the old "closed" system did.

For one thing, the individual members of both houses are significantly more independent of the leaders' rewards, punishments, and requests than they used to be. Where once it was highly unusual, now it is quite common for a committee's recommendations to be ignored or overridden by the whole chamber. That means that there is no longer a small group of powerful leaders in either chamber who know what is going on and who can predict—let alone control—how their chamber will go on most matters. And that, in turn, means that there is no small group of leaders with whom the president can negotiate, make a bargain, and know that Congress's side of the bargain will be kept. Rather, in Ornstein's words:

> ... the open system requires much more frequent use of the most precious presidential resource—the president himself. Telephone calls to wavering members, meetings with important congressional groups, intimate give-and-take sessions with important legislators, close working arrangements with congressional leaders are all necessary to maintain the broad net of relationships a president needs in Congress to get things done. A president who wishes to be successful with Congress will be willing to commit precious personal time to persuading members, and will carry out the task of persuasion eagerly and cheerfully.[20]

If he enjoys that sort of thing and is good at it, as Ronald Reagan is said to be, then he can get a lot done. But if he finds it hard to cozy up to congressmen and would prefer to lecture them, as Jimmy Carter is said to have done, he will find it a lot harder than presidents did in the days of "closed" Congresses to get his programs adopted.

In short, Congress and individual congressmen get a lot more attention from television and the other media in the

Governing in the Television Age

1980s than they did in the 1960s and earlier. For most members this makes life more exciting—and also more wearing and more dangerous—than it used to be. And it makes Congress as an institution more open to the cameras' stare and the correspondents' comments, more active, more fragmented, and less able to form lasting coalitions and mount comprehensive, consistent, and sustained programs. As an Ornstein analogy put it, "the new Congress is an anthill of activity, but that means much motion and little movement."[21]

However, television's needs for a steady stream of newsworthy interviews with interesting congressmen are fulfilled just as well, if not better, by motion as by movement. And since Congress is made up entirely of politicians, how could anyone who gets his political information mainly from television expect anything else from a body composed of people like that?

Political Parties. In chapter 4 we considered at some length the traditional coalition-building role of our national political parties, the steady decline since the 1960s of their ability to play that role, and the part that television has played in that decline. The consequence is that we can no longer look to the parties to pull together the government's policy-making process when the president and Congress fail to do so. It is difficult to see who will.

Shortening Elective Tenures

We noted earlier that no president since Dwight Eisenhower (1953–1961) has served two full terms in office and that in the two most recent presidential elections the incumbents were defeated. It is too early to say with certainty, but presidents seem to be more vulnerable in the television age then they were before, and it may be that in the future it will be just as unusual for an incumbent president to be reelected as it used to be for one to be defeated.

But is this situation unique to presidents, or does it apply to members of Congress as well? Part of the answer is supplied by the data in table 5.1.

TABLE 5.1
Retirements and Electoral Defeats of Incumbent Representatives and Senators, 1952-1980

Period	Percentage of Incumbents Retiring		Percentage of Incumbents Seeking Reelection Defeated in Elections	
	Representatives	Senators	Representatives	Senators
1952-1960	6.7	5.6	7.8	22.7
1962-1970	6.0	3.8	8.5	19.2
1972-1980	9.8	7.2	7.7	32.3

SOURCE: Norman J. Ornstein, Thomas E. Mann, Michael J. Malbin, and John F. Bibby, *Vital Statistics on Congress, 1982* (Washington, D.C.: American Enterprise Institute, 1982), Tables 2-7 and 2-8, pp. 46-48.

The data in table 5.1 show that the electoral vulnerability of U.S. representatives has changed very little in the three decades of the television age. On the other hand, the vulnerability of U.S. senators declined somewhat in the 1960s, but rose sharply in the 1970s. Despite the better showing of incumbent senators in the 1982 election (only 7 percent seeking reelection lost, although several more came very close to defeat), it seems likely that senators have become more vulnerable than representatives and that their greater vulnerability is due in part to their greater television exposure and visibility.

Perhaps the most interesting figures in table 5.1 are those concerning the retirement rates of incumbents in both houses, where it declined somewhat in both houses the 1960s but rose sharply in both in the 1970s. This is no doubt due in part to

Governing in the Television Age

the improvement in congressmen's pensions and other retirement benefits, but there are other reasons as well. As Thomas Mann points out:

> The reasons for the increase in retirements since 1972 are diverse: the job is much tougher, the life is less pleasant, the pace is excruciating, the rewards for longevity are reduced, and the financial incentives to leave are greater, particularly since retirement benefits have been sweetened and congressional salaries have failed to keep pace with inflation.[22]

On the basis of extensive interviews with U.S. representatives, house staff members, and Capitol Hill reporters, Michael Robinson has concluded that the coverage of Congress by the press, particularly by television, has also played a major role in making Congress an even less respected institution than it used to be. He notes that when the Supreme Court in 1976 gave Congress thirty days in which to reconstitute the Federal Election Commission, a leading television commentator, David Brinkley, typified the broadcasters' perspective with his on-the-air remark that "It is widely believed in Washington that it would take Congress thirty days to make instant coffee."[23]

Robinson also points out that the national network news programs focus on the Congress as an institution much more than on its individual members (unless, like Edward Kennedy, they are strong presidential possibilities) and treat the institution with something close to contempt. The local newscasters, on the other hand, concentrate almost entirely on their local congressmen and generally treat them very well. By contrast, the national networks treat the institution of the presidency with great respect, but frequently point out how poorly the current incumbent is filling that great office.[24]

Television's different treatment of the two branches and their incumbents, Robinson concludes, has several major consequences. One is the widely-remarked paradox evident in public opinion polls that most people think quite well of their own congressmen but very poorly of Congress as an institution. Another is the fact that the increasingly powerful requirement that successful candidates for Congress be "good on television" before anything else (a phenomenon we observed in detail in chapter 4) has produced a new kind of congressman:

> ... the increasingly greater reliance on the media for nomination, election, status in the Congress, and reelection is one sign of a new congressional character—one more dynamic, egocentric, immoderate, and, perhaps, intemperate. The evidence here is speculative and thin. But interviews and recent studies indicate that the media ... have recruited, maintained, and promoted a new legislative temperament.

And Robinson quotes a media consultant who has worked on many congressional campaigns this way:

> You ... get the guys with the blow-dried hair who read the script well. That's not the kind of guy who'd been elected to the congress or senate ten years ago. You've got a guy who is not concerned about issues; who isn't concerned about the mechanics of government; who doesn't attend committee meetings; who avoids taking positions at any opportunity and who yet is a master at getting his face in the newspapers and on television....[25]

Weaker Congressmen and Presidents— Stronger Bureaucrats

FILLING THE CONGRESSIONAL VACUUM

Robinson concludes that the new style of congressman operating in the new "open" Congress leads to this paradoxical result:

Governing in the Television Age

In a final irony the modern media in Congress mean that although more policy information is directly available to members than ever before, the members themselves spend no more time with that information than they ever did. Public relations, after all, has become more and more demanding on the members' time. *Policy can be more efficiently handled by staff or subcommittee.*[*][26]

Other observers have made the same point. The early retirements and electoral vulnerability of incumbents and their necessarily greater concentration on their public images—all encouraged if not exclusively caused by television's coverage—means that they have less time, energy, and even inclination to operate the complex governing machinery of Congress. It is said that it takes a congressman at least one term just to find out where all the hideaway offices in the Capitol are, let alone learn how to operate effectively in the committee rooms, cloakrooms, and on the floor. Moreover, the shorter the time congressmen have been in office the less likely they are to know each other well personally, learn who wants to help govern and who wants only to keep his constituents happy, learn who is smart and who is not, and learn who is worth approaching and who is not when one is trying to build a coalition.

The general weakening of congressmen's concern for and expertise in the substance of policy issues leaves a vacuum. That vacuum must be filled by someone; Congress's policymaking business must be conducted somehow. And in the past decade or so that vacuum has been filled more and more by congressional staff—the "unelected representatives" about whom Michael Malbin has written.[27] He points out that they constitute a powerful and rapidly growing bureaucracy: in 1947 there were only 2,030 personal staff and 399 committee staff members; in 1972 the numbers had grown to 7,706 and

*Emphasis added.

1,661; and in 1979 there were 10,679 and 3,057—well over a 300 percent increase in just thirty-two years.[28] And although, like the members of any bureaucracy in a democracy, they are formally subordinate to the elected members, their actual role in Congress's policy-making work is enormous and growing. Malbin sums it up:

> In principle, of course, the members hire, fire, and therefore control their staffs. Nevertheless, the staff exercises a great deal of indirect influence over which the members' control is at best tenuous and imperfect. That influence arises from the simple fact that the members have more to do than time in which to do it.... For example, [the staffs'] ability to run committee investigations, the results of which they can skillfully leak to the media, gives them influence over the items members choose to put on the legislative agenda. Once a bill is on the agenda, the staff works to assemble a coalition behind it, arranging detailed amendments with other staff members and with interest group representatives to broaden support for the bill without sacrificing the goals the chairman, often at their urging, has adopted. When conflicts cannot be resolved, the members may then learn enough about the details to weigh the political costs of compromise. But even then, the role of the member is clearly limited. As former Senator Dick Clark (D–Iowa) once said: "There is no question about our enormous dependency and their influence. In all legislation, they're the ones that lay out the options."[29]

FILLING THE PRESIDENTIAL VACUUM

The fantasy of an all-powerful chief executive enthroned at the top of an ordered hierarchy of departments, bureaus, and agencies issuing orders that are rapidly received and faithfully executed has long since evaporated under the hard light of dozens of reports by presidents and thousands of analyses by scholars.[30] Even so, many observers say that the power of presidents in recent years, especially since the mid–1970s, has declined significantly, and some believe, as I do, that television has had an important, though not an exclusive or perhaps even primary, role in that process.

My reasoning is simple: political nature abhors a vacuum in the executive branch every bit as much as one in the legislative branch. Hence to the extent that a president has to spend more of his limited time and energy dealing with his vast public relations problems, exacerbated as they are by the adversarial way in which television and the press contrast the feebleness of his performance with the greatness of the office, the less time he has to spend on everything else. And "everything else" includes the Jovian task of deciding what are the best policies to pursue and the Herculean task of trying to get the executive agencies to do what he wants them to do.

Upper level career civil servants are, of course, no more unanimous in their policy preferences than are elected officials, and the political struggles among them over whose programs will become the policies urged on the president and his advisors by the departments, bureaus, and agencies are at least as strenuous as those between Democratic and Republican candidates and officeholders.[31]

Television, however, gives bureaucratic politics only a tiny fraction of the coverage it gives to the politics of the president, his top advisors, and the Congress. There are several reasons for this discrepancy. For one thing, bureaucrats do not run for office or conduct open campaigns yielding "good visuals" easily captured by film crews. Their struggles take place in obscure offices and corridors, and they do not provide recurring and easily available "scores" comparable to those provided by the poll results and election returns so necessary for the networks' "horse race" journalism coverage of electoral politics.

For another thing, where elected politicians need and seek as much good television coverage as possible, bureaucratic politicians need and seek as much inattention from the mass media as they can manage. As we observed in chapter 4, while bureaucrats frequently leak information to reporters as one way of advancing their personal interests and policy preferences, they demand, and almost always get, anonymity as their principal price for making it so easy for reporters to get the information. And most reporters, whether working for television or newspapers, are only too glad to protect their sources even though that means that they can cover only a small part—mainly the part played by elected officials—of the whole policy-making process. A bureaucrat caught red-handed taking a bribe or stealing public property or demanding sexual favors from subordinates will certainly draw the attention of television and the other media; indeed, such personal scandals are among the medias' most broadcast and published stories. But the far more numerous, complex, and important struggles among bureaucrats over policy questions remain almost as unknown to television audiences as the behind-the-camera struggles among network executives over broadcasting policies.

The viewers might find such stories at least as entertaining and informative as the present flood of stories about the politics of elections and elected officials; but in the foreseeable future they are not likely to get them, or very many of them, on the nightly newscasts.

Conclusion

All of the ways in which the American way of government has changed since the end of World War II certainly cannot be blamed (or credited) solely or perhaps even mainly on the advent of television. But if there is any merit in the argument of the foregoing pages, it seems clear that the glare of television's attention has helped significantly to weaken the ability of presidents and congressmen to govern. It seems equally

Governing in the Television Age

clear that television's relative inattention to bureaucratic politics has significantly helped the unelected officials in both the legislative and executive branches to fill the policy-making vacuums left by the declining power of the elected officials.

In a world in which political reality for most Americans consists mostly of what they see on television, how could it be otherwise?

Chapter 6

On Balance

IN the preceding chapter I have tried to describe the impact of television on American politics from the late 1940s to the mid-1980s. In this concluding chapter, I propose to use a wider-angle lens to consider three questions by way of summing up: Is the new technology likely to alter significantly television's impact on our politics? Is its present impact, on balance, good or bad for our political system? Are there ways in which that impact can be made more benign?

New Technology, New Impact?

THE PROLIFERATION OF VIEWERS' CHOICES

We have observed repeatedly in earlier chapters that one of the prime characteristics of the television age has been the three national networks' near monopoly of the viewing audience and, consequently, of the portrayal of politics for most Americans. During most of the period, the stations affiliated with ABC, CBS, and NBC have together attracted about 90

On Balance

percent of the viewers, with the remainder left to independent commercial stations and public stations affiliated with the Public Broadcasting Service (PBS). The networks' corner on the broadcasting of national news has been even greater. The only regularly-broadcast nonnetwork national news show has been PBS's "MacNeil/Lehrer Report," and it is aired at times that do not compete directly with the network newscasts. The networks' local affiliates and local independent stations, to be sure, devote a lot of money and broadcast time to news-weather-and-sports shows they produce themselves (indeed, these are about the only shows on which the local stations spend much production money). But these local shows have fewer political stories than the national newscasts, and what national political stories they do broadcast are taken almost entirely from the networks' feeds. Moreover, the national news shows have had relatively large audiences: for example, in the last week of 1982, "CBS Evening News" drew 26 percent of the entire viewing audience, "NBC Nightly News" had a 22-percent share, and "ABC World News Tonight" also had a 22-percent share—for a total share of 70 percent for the three combined.[1]

Audience surveys show, however, that the networks' share of the prime-time audience for all programming has been dropping in recent years. In the 1960s and 1970s it was about 90 percent, but in the mid-1980s it has dropped to about 80 percent. Some informed observers believe that it will drop even further, perhaps as low as 60 percent or even less by the 1990s.[2] The main reason for the networks' slippage has been the proliferation of alternatives offered viewers by television's new technology, and some observers expect that technology will produce further major changes in the industry's structure and in people's viewing habits in the 1980s and 1990s.

The most important effect of the new technology is expected to be the much greater number of program choices available to viewers. Most viewers in the 1960s and 1970s had, at most, five or six choices from standard broadcasting—the local affiliates of the three networks, perhaps a local public station, and perhaps a local independent commercial station or two. But the new technology is capable of offering viewers many more choices, perhaps more than 100 in all.

Several new devices and services are expected to multiply the choices. One is the steady increase in pay-television services, such as Home Box Office. Evidently a growing number of viewers are willing to pay a monthly fee in order to see the sports, movies, and other programs they want without having to depend on the networks' programming or having to watch the commercials that pay for "free" television.

Another device is direct satellite broadcasting, in which a nonnetwork broadcaster beams a signal to a communications satellite where it is amplified and reflected back to earth where it can be received by any person with a dish-antenna on his roof or in his back yard and unscrambled by a device attached to his set. Satellite broadcasting will not be ready for general home use until the late 1980s or early 1990s, but it could drain away the networks' audiences even more.

Still another device is the videocassette recorder (VCR), which allows viewers to copy any broadcast program they wish and see it later, or to purchase or rent videotapes of theater movies, sports events, and the like. Videodisc players enable viewers to play prerecorded movies and other programs, though not to make their own recordings. At the present writing there is a legal contest over whether the home recording of broadcast programs is a violation of copyright laws. The result could conceivably be that all such recording will be outlawed, but the more likely result is that viewers will have to pay some modest royalties, perhaps in the form of higher prices for blank videocassettes. If so, VCRs will continue to provide yet another alternative to watching the networks.

Cable television, however, is generally considered to be the device that will most increase the viewers' choices. It was first used in the 1960s in rural areas so remote from the broadcast transmitters in urban areas that they were able to receive only weak and snowy signals. The first cable companies built huge antennas that effectively received weak and distant signals, and, for a fee, transmitted the amplified signals by cables directly wired to people's homes. This not only improved reception, it also gave the subscribers considerably more channels to watch than were provided by unwired broadcasting of the traditional variety.

Since then cable technology has improved and the number of subscribers has greatly increased. By using fibre optics instead of conventional cables and by improving the receiving capabilities of home receivers, it is now technically feasible to offer as many as 108 channels; 54 channels are expected to be the standard number offered to most cable users in the future.[3] In 1982, the total number of households subscribing to some kind of cable service was estimated to be 27 million; and some analysts predict that by 1990 the number will rise to 55 or 60 million, or about 80 percent of all homes.[4] Some observers, with a tip of the hat (or a thumb of the nose) to Charles Reich, call this development "the wiring of America."[5]

Whatever it is called, the rapid expansion of the cable industry will provide more and more Americans with many more viewing choices than they have ever had before. Furthermore, cable technology allows signals to be transmitted from home to station as well as from station to home, and this has made possible what is known in the trade as "interactive television." As it operates in the well-known "Qube" system established experimentally in Columbus, Ohio, by Warner Communications, all cable subscribers can have a device connected to their receivers that enables them to transmit signals back to the broadcaster. For example, a channel broadcasts a discussion of a political issue, say the issue of abortion. After it concludes, the viewers are requested to register their own opinions. The announcer, reinforced by graphics on the screen, says, "If you favor leaving the decisions about abortions entirely to the woman involved, press button '1'; if you favor the Supreme Court's present policy of allowing abortions only at certain periods of pregnancy, press button '2'; if you favor a constitutional amendment prohibiting abortions in any circumstances, press button '3'; if you favor each state deciding the matter for itself, press button '4'. Please press your button now." The subscribers push the appropriate buttons, the signals travel along the cable back to the studio where they are tabulated by computers, and the results are announced.

Some analysts see interactive television as the brave new device that will provide rapid, cheap, and practical home referendums on public issues, thereby realizing the old dream of town-meeting-style direct democracy for millions of citizens, perhaps even for the national electorate. For example, Kas Kalba predicts:

> An alteration of our political system is . . . likely to occur in tomorrow's electronic community. Channel abundance will allow the home viewer to follow local town council or PTA proceedings. Feedback mechanisms will permit him to register an opinion at these proceedings or to vote in national referenda.[6]

Some people may find Kalba's vision either fanciful or frightening. But no matter how much or how little interactive television is used, it is likely that by the 1990s most American will have fifty or more channels to watch rather than the five or six they have now.

AN END TO THE NETWORKS' POLITICAL DOMINANCE?

Some analysts believe that the new technology's "channel abundance" will effectively end the networks' long-standing dominance over the portrayal of politics. If they are correct,

On Balance

then most of this book's observations will be out of date and irrelevant by the 1990s.

Now, as a citizen, I might welcome that turn of events; as an author, I might regret its timing; but as an observer, I do not believe that the networks' near monopoly over the depiction of politics will be greatly weakened no matter how many channels viewers can tune in.

To be sure, there is no technical reason why, in addition to the network newscasts, we cannot also have a number of other channels broadcasting news and presenting different portraits of political reality. For instance, not only might we have more news and political programs by commercial and noncommercial broadcasters, but political interest groups could also operate their own channels. The new technology will certainly permit channels to be operated by such organizations as the Democratic and Republican parties, the Americans for Democratic Action, the National Conservative Political Action Committee, the National Organization for Women, the Moral Majority, and so on and on. After all, 35 channels will provide a lot of network bypasses, and 108 channels would provide a lot more. But will they be used for political broadcasting? That is the key question, and the answer, I believe, is: not much.

The expectation that political groups will use a lot of the new channels to broadcast political news as they feel it should be presented rests upon the assumption that there are millions of viewers out there who are hungry for political information, who are turned off by the superficiality or the bias of the networks' political stories, and who would, by the millions, tune in channels that deal with politics "fairly"—that is, channels, that are more favorable to liberals, conservatives, Democrats, Republicans, or whatever parties and causes particular viewers favor. After all, some say, the emergence of the new cable-based all-news networks, such as C-SPAN (Cable-Satellite Public Affairs Network) and CNN (Ted Turner's Cable News

Network), indicates the desire of millions of viewers for more and better news. And to meet the competition some of the networks have already scheduled additional news shows for the early morning hours, for example, "NBC News Overnight" (1:30–2:30 A.M. Eastern time).

Before we hail the blooming of a thousand new flowers in television's presentation of political news, however, let us remember that none of the existing alternative news shows have more than a small fraction of the audience watching the networks' regular nightly newscasts. We can be sure that what audiences the alternative news shows do have are composed almost entirely of "political buffs" and "news junkies." And they, as we saw in chapter 3, are not only a small minority of the population, but, precisely because they are so interested in politics and acquire so much political information, they are also likely to come to the tube with strongly-held, preconceived political views and are therefore not likely to have their perceptions of political reality shaped solely or even mainly by television, no matter how many channels it offers.

What the cable industry is presently doing with its abundance of new channels offers a clue as to how they will be used in the future. Most of them broadcast reruns of popular network entertainment shows, such as "M*A*S*H" and "Happy Days," sports of all kinds, the same old movies the networks show, and the X–rated movies the networks do not show. There is every reason to believe that "Joe Six-Pack" (today's descendant of the mythical average man the newspapers used to call "John Q. Public") will continue to make up the great majority of the viewing audience. And while his fifty-four channels may provide him with several new all-news and heavy-on-politics channels as well as more sit-coms, cop shows, and sportscasts, he is not likely to choose the Democrats' channel or the Moral Majority's channel or (*pace* Kas Kalba) the community channel broadcasting live meetings of

On Balance

the city council or the PTA. What political information he gets he will continue to get because he happens to be watching television while short political stories are being broadcast or because he occasionally tunes in a broadcast of an especially interesting political event, such as a presidential debate. Those will give him all the political information he wants, and he will be no more inclined to seek out a lot more than he has ever been.

MOBILIZING INTEREST GROUPS

For these reasons, I do not believe that television's new channel abundance will significantly reduce the three networks' well-established near monopoly over the presentation of political news, or the shaping of political reality for the great majority of Americans who make up the "inadvertent audience."

That is not to say, however, that the new technology will have no political impact at all. Its main effect may well be to improve the effectiveness and increase the power of special interest groups. In times past when the Washington representatives of such a group decided that some impending action by the Congress or an administrative agency would strongly promote or damage the group's interests, they would often send "red alert" messages by letters and telegrams to their members around the country urging them to put special pressure on the key public officials to support or oppose the bill or regulation in question.

At present, a growing number of special interest groups, such as the United States Chamber of Commerce, are using cable and satellite technology to send "red alerts" to local meetings of their members to mobilize them for action. Warnings signaled in this way appear to be considerably more effective in stirring the members to act than those communicated by the old-fashioned methods, and it seems likely that in the future more and more groups will use these new techniques.

If they do, the political impact might be considerable. In chapters 4 and 5 we reviewed the decline of the parties and other coalition-building agencies in the age of television, and noted that much of the resulting political vacuum has been filled by the television networks and by the growing number, power, and intransigence of special interest groups. The new telecommunications techniques are likely to enable these groups to mobilize their members more rapidly and effectively than ever and thereby make the groups even more powerful. Hence the main political impact of television's new devices may be, not to make ordinary citizens better informed, but to fragment the policy-making processes of government even further. We will return to this point later.

If I am correct in believing that the three networks' dominance over the portrayal of politics is likely to continue despite the new technology, then the time has come for me to strike the best balance I can between the good and the harm that that portrayal has done and is likely to continue doing to the American political system.

Television and the American Political System

Before I start handing out merits and demerits to network television, it seems appropriate to repeat once more a caution offered several times in this book: Television, no matter how dramatic may have been its rise or how attention-compelling its pictures, is not now and never has been an all-powerful weapon, a kind of videogame "joystick" control, that enables its producers to create any effects they like. Every political communication situation has a number of elements, each of

On Balance

which play a role in shaping its political consequences. The medium which transmits the messages is only one of those elements, and television is only one such medium.[7]

There is little doubt that for most Americans television is a more powerful mass medium (that is, a method of transmitting a message from a communicator to an audience of tens of thousands or millions) than newspapers, radio, magazines, books, or movies. Its pictures and sounds simulate life and compel attention much more than do radio's sounds or the words of newspapers, books, or magazines. So television's attractively illustrated stories, news and fiction, viewed with little effort in one's own home have given the medium a preeminence among the mass media that it is not likely to lose.

But several other factors also affect the impact of political communications. One is the communicator: If he is perceived as a familiar, likeable, trustworthy, "cool" person (such as, for example, Walter Cronkite or Ronald Reagan), he is likely to be considerably more effective than one who is unknown or too "hot" or too shifty (readers will supply their own illustrations). Another factor is the message's content: If it comes across as an accurate presentation of the facts and a balanced presentation of the competing views, it will be far more convincing than if it is seen as naked advocacy of one side. And another factor is the audience: If the message deals with matters about which the viewers already hold strong views (such as, for example, whether women should be allowed to have abortions whenever they wish), any message, no matter how well written and effectively delivered, is not likely to change many viewers' minds. But if the message deals with a matter about which the viewers know little and care less (for example, the use of the basing-point system for antitrust prosecutions), a well-presented broadcast may well make up many minds—if, that is, the viewers can be persuaded to watch the broadcast at all. Many studies have shown that less-educated, poorer people depend more on television for learning about what is going on in the world than better-educated, richer people do; and, knowing less, they are likely to be influenced more.

Still another factor is the message's costs. A message that asks viewers to do something—to contribute their money or vote or attend a political rally—is less likely to achieve its goal than one that asks viewers merely to "believe" something without having to stir from their armchairs.

Perhaps the most important factor of all is the context. Does the communication fit well with the audience's established perceptions of the real state of affairs, or does it seem to ignore or contradict them? For example, the Republicans' well-produced televised advertisements in the 1982 congressional campaigns about how the economy was recovering and how the Reagan program was working well were much better received by investors who were doing well in New York's "bull" stock market than by unemployed auto workers in Detroit—same message, same medium, different audiences, different contexts, different results. Moreover, even if, as I have been saying throughout this book, television is the most important source of political reality for most Americans, it still is not the only source, even for the less-educated and poor. They watch a lot of television, yes, but they still get some information and attitudes from their families, friends, and workmates, from newspapers and radios, and from the sights and sounds of their everyday lives.

In short, although I can and now will try to assess the good and bad effects that television has had upon the American political system, I cannot say in any instance that television is the sole, or even clearly the most important, cause of the effects that I like or dislike. With that important qualification in mind, let us turn, at last, to an evaluation of television's impact on American politics.

Television has certainly brought some substantial benefits to our political system. For instance, it is all but impossible

On Balance

today for a nationally ambitious politician to take one stand in one part of the country and quite a different stand in another part. The cameras and microphones record his public utterances almost everywhere, and the networks' newspeople are always eager to point out any politician's inconsistencies, especially if they are seen to stem from his willingness to say anything anywhere if he thinks it will win votes and campaign contributions. That makes it much harder than it once was for such politicians to play different regions off against one another, and that is certainly a benefit.

For another instance, television at its best can bring to its viewers a vivid sense that they are seeing the true facts in a political conflict of crisis proportions, and that can give the conflict's resolution a legitimacy it might otherwise lack. Surely one of television's finest hours was its live broadcasts of the House Judiciary Committee's debates on the articles of impeachment against Richard Nixon in 1974. Whatever the millions of viewers may have thought of the committee's ultimate decisions, few doubted the evidence of their own eyes and ears that this divisive and dangerous issue was being decided by conscientious, intelligent, hardworking, and fairminded congressmen from both parties and on both sides of the issue. And surely the resulting public confidence in the legitimacy of the decisionmaking process played a major role in the nation's calm acceptance of a decision that under other circumstances might have left disfiguring scars.

Let us remember that the people who create the networks' newscasts—presidents of news divisions, executive producers, producers of particular news shows, correspondents, and anchors—are often called on to defend the way they do their jobs against the criticisms of people like me who are outside the business. To their continuing credit, the newspeople often respond. When they do, they generally say something like this: Despite the show-biz aspects of their business (most of which they deplore as much as we do), they are essentially reporters, just as much as the people who work for the *New York Times* or *Wall Street Journal*. As reporters, they have one prime professional obligation that overrides all others: their job is to find out what is really happening in the world and tell their viewers about it. Of course, like their colleagues in print journalism, they have to report the news in ways that will make it comprehensible and interesting to their audiences. But telling it like it is—that is the core of their job.

They recognize that other people have different jobs. Take politicians, for example. Their job is to get elected or reelected, to get their programs adopted, and to keep the voters happy. They know how much the people trust television news, and so they are constantly trying to use the news to help them persuade the voters that they are doing the right things. Television newspeople understand that, and they use every safeguard they can to keep themselves from being used for some politician's advantage. It is not part of their job to help government programs work more smoothly or make any politician's life easier, even if he is president of the United States. The newscasters' job is to tell their viewers—most of whom could never find out for themselves—what the government is really doing, what its real reasons are for doing so, and whether it is really working or not. As one print journalist so pointedly put it, "I think it's [the government's] job . . . to keep secrets. . . . My job is to find them." CBS anchorman Dan Rather added, "As a professional, my job is to publish and be damned."[8] And Rather's great predecessor, Walter Cronkite, summed up this view in the clearest possible words:

> I don't think it is any of our business what the moral, political, social or economic effort of our reporting is. I say let's get on with the job of reporting the news—and let the chips fall where they may.[9]

Finally, television people feel that they do their job pretty well, especially considering how little time they have, how

On Balance

high their production costs are, and how cramped they are by government regulations such as the fairness doctrine. Because so many more people watch and trust television news than read and trust newspapers, newscasters can fairly claim a lot of the credit for the fact that the American people know a lot more about public affairs—and are a lot less hoodwinked by politicians—than they used to be.

There is a good deal of merit in this defense. We noted in chapter 1 that most Americans report that they get more of their political information from television than from newspapers, radio, magazines, personal conversations, or any other source; moreover, they trust the information they get from television more than they trust what they get from any other source. Many studies by social scientists confirm this.[10] Moreover, the studies also show that the less formal education and the lower social status people have, the greater is their dependence on television for political information and understanding. And if there were no televising of political information whatever, many more Americans would know even less about politics than they do now.

Some critics respond to this argument by repeating the old maxim that "a little knowledge is a dangerous thing." Perhaps so, the newscasters reply, but in a democracy no knowledge at all is even more dangerous. Other critics say that the kind of political information television imparts is not real knowledge at all—it is only a random scattering of "factlets" pumped out indiscriminately by the networks so that they jostle around meaninglessly in the viewers' minds. But that charge, I think, is wide of the mark. Television newspeople certainly try their best to present each show's collection of stories and facts, old and new, as part of some theme that their viewers will recognize and find meaningful. And that, in my view, raises quite a different problem for the health of the political system.

Throughout this book I have tried to make clear my view that television newspeople are not conspirators or miscreants.

Few if any of them deliberately use their positions to advance particular ideologies, causes, candidates, or parties. Few if any lack concern for the welfare of their country or its political system and focus solely on how they can get the big jobs, the big ratings, and the big budgets. Nothing infuriates them more than to be told that they are in "show business." They feel that they are journalists just as much as the people who work for the newspapers or the news magazines. And with few exceptions they are as conscientious, hardworking, and dedicated to high standards as other journalists. Most of them feel that they operate under considerably greater handicaps than print journalism—for example, the brief flashes of air time in which they must report their stories, the need to make the stories pictorially interesting, the lack of time and money to do their own investigative reporting, the inhibitions of the fairness doctrine, and so on.

Despite these handicaps, most of them try their best to live up to what they see as the highest standards of journalism. But their perceptions of those standards have, in my view, led to several undesirable consequences.

Take, for example, the broadcasters' prevailing ideas about what constitutes "news." News, as they conceive it, consists of happenings—what people have said and done. Moreover, news is, by definition, what has happened recently, usually in the twenty-four hours since the last nightly newscast or even the six and a half hours since the noon newscasts. Of course only a small fraction of those happenings can be reported in any half-hour news show, so only the most newsworthy can be put on the air. And which are those? For the most part they are the items that can most easily be presented as parts of ongoing stories and themes with which viewers are already familiar, and the items that can be presented as especially important or especially deserving of the viewers' attention.[11]

This conception of news underlies just about everything that television newspeople do, and it accounts for many of the

On Balance

more harmful effects of their efforts. For instance, in chapter 3 we discussed the "information avalanche" and its consequences. Night after night, almost every political story is trumpeted as important, and after awhile the viewers' eyes glaze, their senses numb, and if everything is important then nothing is important. The correspondents and the anchors have cried "wolf" (or "liar" or "thief") just too often.

For another instance, the "horse race" journalism approach that so dominates television's political reporting inevitably leads to eagerness for scoops and for "scores" to report and dramatize every night. And that, in turn, builds in the viewers' minds a picture of politics and government as a bewildering succession of upward zooms and downward plunges rather than the much slower crabwise movement from one compromise to the next that most politicians believe they are involved in.

For still another instance, the conception of "news" that underlies most television and newspaper reporting tends to make the abnormal in government change places with the normal. I cannot recall a single network story (and only a few newspaper features) that said, in effect, "Today 533 of 535 members of Congress read their newspapers, answered their mail, attended their committee meetings, studied bills, consulted with their staffs, showed constituents around, spoke on the floor, reached some compromises with other members, attended diplomatic receptions, and collapsed in bed." That in fact is normal, but it is not news as newspapers or television news show report it. Their news is: "Today, two members of Congress were accused of (indicted for, convicted of) taking bribes." The occasional scandalous acts of a few public officials get a lot of exposure because they are news, while the far more common conscientious performance of their duties by almost all public officials gets little or no television exposure. That may be what they do, but it is not news. All perfectly understandable, no doubt; but when the viewers see many more interesting stories about the abnormal scandals than about the normal good behavior, it is not surprising that they come to believe, as they did about the Watergate scandals, that "all politicians do it, but only some get caught."

Permeating this and just about everything else they do is the newscasters' conviction, which they certainly share with most print journalists, that their profession requires them to take an adversarial posture toward politicians and public officials. Many feel, indeed, that their position as the people's watchdogs is the basic justification for their place in society and the many rewards of high salaries and personal fame it brings for its top people. The newscasters' view, as we have often observed, is that it is the politicians' job to develop, sell, and implement policies that will deal with the nation's problems and also to keep secrets if they think it will make their tasks easier. But it is the journalist's job to ferret out those secrets, dramatize the conflicts over the policies, expose the flaws in the results, and tell the American people all the things they could never find out for themselves about the politicians' wheeling and dealing, lying, and cheating.

The Consequences

In chapters 3, 4, and 5, I have detailed what I believe to be the consequences of television's portrayal of politics for the American political system. I shall list them only summarily here.

The avalanche of "important" political stories beamed at viewers who are not much interested in politics confirms their view that politics is confusing and boring, and that politicians are liars, blowhards, and hypocrites. So the viewers grow less and less inclined to vote for one set of politicians over another, especially since government never seems to do much good for very long no matter which gang gets in.

On Balance

Television's domination of primary and general election campaigns has made it more and more difficult for anyone who is not "good on television" to be nominated and elected to office; and the qualities that make people good on television are only randomly related to the qualities that make people good at governing. If we get some skillful television performers who also become excellent presidents, senators, and representatives, it will be because we are lucky, not because good performance on the tube is a good predictor of good performance in office.

The networks' constant focus on scandals and their steady denigration of politicians and political parties has helped to make our traditionally low opinion of politicians even lower.

The networks' news decisions about which aspirants for presidential nominations have a serious chance and which do not make them, willy nilly, participants in the political process—for those decisions have far more influence on who can stay in the race and who cannot than any judgments made by other politicians.

The networks' need to fill their newscasts night after night with new and attention-catching stories has speeded up political time: it has inflated politicians' rhetoric and people's expectations about what government can do; and it has reduced the time politicians have to put their programs in place and show results that will meet those expectations.

As a result, elected public officials, from presidents on down, are portrayed and perceived as successes much less frequently than they were before the television age. They have less influence as leaders, and their political lives are less fun. More of them decide to retire earlier from their offices. And the general weakening of elected officials' power has created a vacuum largely filled by unelected officials, such as bureaucrats and congressional staffs, who, not coincidentally, get much less attention from the media than do their elected nominal superiors.

In short, television has raised ordinary people's expectations of what government can and should do, but has made it more difficult for those who govern to meet those expectations. And it has also made most government achievements seem transitory, unimportant, or even illusory. Government has become weaker in the age of television, and the networks' portrayal of politics has played a significant role in that weakening.

However, it is important to recognize that whatever effect television has had along these lines is not a transformation of what government in America is intended to be and once was. Television's effect has been, rather, to intensify most of the fundamental characteristics of our system of government as planned by the Founding Fathers and nurtured by much of American tradition. That tradition, as we noted earlier, fears most the danger that government will grow too powerful and that its power will be seized by factions bent on advancing their selfish interests at the expense of the general interest. Government must therefore be constantly watched, the secret machinations of the factions grasping for its power must be exposed, and any government action that offends any major segment of the community must be stopped in its tracks.

Television newscasters are well steeped in that tradition, especially in its post-1960s neo-progressive version, and most of what they do perpetuates and intensifies it. Consequently, it seems reasonable to suppose that if the networks' nightly newscasts could somehow be beamed to the Founding Fathers (query without answer: would a true Paradise have television or not?), they might be put off by its show-biz trappings, but they would not, I think, be displeased by many of its effects upon the system of government they designed. For whatever else television may or may not have done, it has certainly become a potent new force helping to keep government and the elected politicians who are supposed to run it from becoming too powerful. We have paid a price, of course. The price is that it is even more difficult in the 1980s than it was before the

On Balance

television age for the president or Congress to install and sustain a coherent program of any kind that involves any sudden and substantial departure from what the government is already doing. The Reagan administration, after its early and heady success in 1981, seems to have learned this hard fact of life just as the Carter, Ford, Nixon, Johnson, and Kennedy administrations had learned it earlier in the television age.

Television's portrayal of politics, in short, has not departed from the American tradition. Rather it has helped greatly to perpetuate it and to intensify its effects.

What To Do and What Not To Do

Like many other outsiders who criticize this or that aspect of the way television portrays politics and paint what some may see as a gloomy picture of its impact on the American political system, I am sometimes asked: What can be done to improve television's political coverage and temper its harmful effects on our politics? It is a fair question, and I shall offer a few answers to it. But I must begin by mentioning some things that I do not believe can or should be done.

I do not, for example, think that things would improve if we somehow got "better people" producing television news—presumably, that is, people who would portray politics as the critics of television would portray it if they were themselves on the air. Most of the people who now produce the network news shows are very good people. Their honesty, intelligence, energy, and dedication to what they regard as the highest standards of their craft certainly match those of, say, print journalists, business executives, college professors, and think tank researchers. Moreover, the people who put together the newscasts in other democracies, such as Canada, France, and Great Britain, are said to be of about the same quality. In short, the newscasters who present politics in America are at least as good as their counterparts elsewhere, and firing the whole lot is no way to improve what television does.

For another thing, I do not believe, for reasons given earlier in this chapter, that the proliferation of channels resulting from the expansion of cable and satellite television will significantly cut into the three major networks' near monopoly over the presentation of political reality.

Finally, I do not believe that closer regulation by the Federal Communications Commission is likely to produce benefits worth the cost of further abridgement of the broadcasters' First Amendment rights. On the other hand, I am also doubtful that the near-total deregulation proposed to Congress by FCC Chairman Mark Fowler in 1981 would produce the greater justice to broadcasters and better television for viewers that he claims it would. And I am convinced that any law prohibiting certain network practices—for example, a law prohibiting the networks from forecasting election outcomes before the polls have closed—would be a clear violation of the First Amendment. So the few suggestions I have are all for changes the networks would have to make themselves, voluntarily and in their own interests as well as the public interest.

Several years ago, Douglass Cater, a man with long experience in both journalism and government, and one of television's most perceptive critics, made this suggestion:

> ... It is time for more public accounting of the problems of news management. How the news is manufactured has been kept a dark mystery even as the media strive to throw the fierce light of publicity on decision making elsewhere. It would be refreshing, first of all, for the public to know that the collecting, processing, and distribution of news requires judgments all along the line. Human judgments. It would be even more helpful to credibility if there were more frank discussions and mutual criticism of human error in the managing of news. For too long the communicators have operated according to Randolph Churchill's dictum that "Dog don't eat dog." When someone commits folly, everyone else looks

On Balance

the other way.... This needs to be carried further. No one can expect self-criticism to be too rigorous. But there is no reason why the newspapers can't be sharply critical of television and television of the print media.[12]

I would go further; I would say that there is no reason why television cannot be sharply critical of television. It is not that the networks never take us behind the scenes to show us something of how they produce their programs. In early 1983, for example, CBS broadcast an informative program about how they choose their entertainment shows. CBS's "60 Minutes" devoted a show to describing how it develops its stories, and so did ABC's "20/20." PBS's series "Inside Story" and ABC's series "Viewpoint" often look critically at how the networks cover the news. But only a handful of the stories on the nightly newscasts deal with television itself.[13]

All of television's programs about television have been well received, and if their ratings were not as high as those for, say, "Dallas" and "The Dukes of Hazzard," they were still respectable. Why not go further? Why not have on each network each week at least one hour of prime time devoted to regular broadcasts about the television business, including its coverage of politics? For example, why not show us how the nightly news is produced—how those in charge decide to broadcast certain stories but not others; how much of the footage available for a particular story is used, what is included and why, what is left out and why? Why not tell us how the network news teams conduct exit polls, draw up key precinct profiles, and make their election night forecasts? Why not give us a discussion of the good and harm, if any, these forecasts do?

Most important of all, why not follow Douglass Cater's suggestion and have each network's regular inside-television broadcasts also critically examine both its own political coverage and the coverage by other networks? If, for example, CBS falls well short of good journalistic practices in its account of how General William Westmoreland conducted the Vietnam

War (as even CBS admitted it did in a 1982 documentary), why not have NBC's or ABC's critic-in-residence say so on the air? And when NBC News or ABC News have comparable lapses, why should not CBS's critics say so on the air?

Television newspeople should remember, in this regard, that these days just about every major newspaper has an "ombudsman." He is a paid member of the staff whose job is to monitor the accuracy and fairness of the paper's news stories. When he decides that a particular story or series of stories is inaccurate or unfair, he writes a column setting forth his objections. The paper has a self-imposed obligation to print it—an obligation the quality papers almost always fulfill. Fair is fair: if television newspeople want to be generally regarded, not as minor entertainers in big show business, but as journalists following the highest standards of their profession, then they have to recognize that ombudsman-style self-criticism has become one of those standards. There is no technical reason why the network news divisions cannot live up to that standard and many good professional reasons why they should.

I do not expect that such regular inside-television programs would have the highest ratings, but I am sure they would have good enough ratings to keep them from becoming economic disasters. They would certainly go far toward answering many of the complaints of television's outside critics, although answering those complaints admittedly may not be very important to the network chiefs. Many of the television newspeople I have talked to are well aware that they do not present political news as well as they might, and many are constantly seeking ways of doing better. I suggest that such programs might be useful in their quest for improvement.

In the end, however, my argument to the network's newspeople is quite simple: practice what you preach. You often admonish your critics that the first obligation of good journalism is to report what is really happening with all the powerful elements of society, not only government but also big corpora-

On Balance

tions, big labor unions, issue groups, and the like. Let the chips fall where they may, you say; our job is to tell it like it is. Fair enough. But surely ABC, CBS, and NBC are also powerful elements of our society, at least as powerful as big oil or big labor or the Democratic and Republican parties. Surely the same professional obligation requires television to tell us about what they themselves and their employers are doing as well as what the nontelevision powerhouses are doing. Or does the journalist's professional obligation to tell it like it is apply only to covering nonjournalists?

I realize that it is probably too much to ask television newspeople to abandon their antipolitician and antiestablishment postures and to highlight the fact that if democratic government is going to operate at all in America it will be operated mainly by politicians. It is equally unlikely that they will portray episodes of negotiation, bargaining, and compromise—wheeling and dealing, if you prefer—as processes vitally necessary for getting the politician's job done. I do not foresee the day in which newscasters will win Peabodys or promotions or the esteem of their peers by telling what terrific jobs some politicians, or politicians in general, are doing to make democracy work. I do not even expect them to start giving the normal as much attention as the abnormal, or to make the honest many "news" as much as the corrupt few are "news," or to confess on the air that most of the stories they are telling so vividly are mere blips in slowly-moving trend lines.

I recognize, moreover, that newscasters in most other democratic countries portray politics in about the same way that American newscasters do. Even though public broadcasting is considerably larger and more powerful in most countries than in the United States, their newscasters nevertheless seem to take very much the same adversarial stance toward politicians and establishments: remember, for example, the conflict between newscasters and the government in Great Britain over the coverage of the Falkland Islands War. It appears, then, that this way of depicting politics is somehow characteristic of the medium itself wherever television is anything more than an arm of a government propaganda ministry. It is certainly not unique to the newscasters of ABC, CBS, and NBC.[14]

Yet we should also note that in many other democratic countries politicians and political parties are, by law or custom, regularly given prime time on television in which to present themselves as they, not the newscasters, decide. Anthony Smith reports that in seventeen of the twenty-one democratic countries he surveyed, free time is given to political parties in all but four to broadcast programs of their own design and production.[15] These programs draw respectable, though not top ratings, and they often evoke skepticism in their viewers similar to that evoked by paid political advertisements in the United States. These days it seems that most veteran viewers are quick to recognize that someone on the tube is trying to sell them something, and most have developed a certain resistance to such messages.

But at least these party broadcasts give the politicians and the parties the chance to present themselves as they see themselves, not as passed through the newscasters' filters and prisms. Is there any good reason why the American networks should not give our parties and politicians similar opportunities? After all, it could not do much harm to the networks or their audiences, and it just might give the politicians a much-needed boost in their public images that would make it easier for them to do what an effective democracy requires them to do.

Conclusion

These modest suggestions, plus more that could no doubt be suggested by television workers and critics more knowledgeable than I, could be of some help. I hope they will be serious-

On Balance

ly considered by those television newscasters, if any, who read this book. Even if such changes are made, however, I expect that television's portrayal of politics is going to remain largely as it has been throughout the television age. If that is the case, then that portrayal will continue to intensify, not transform, the tendencies to fragmenting and scattering political power so carefully built into our constitutional system by its original designers.

After all, the people who do the work of network television do not stand apart from American society. They are reared in American homes, educated in American schools, and live in American culture. They watch a lot of television themselves, if only to see what the competition is doing. Certainly they have an important role in shaping our political culture, but they, like the rest of us, are its products as well.

From all that I can see and understand, Marshall McLuhan and many other students of communication are quite correct in declaring that the advent of television is the most profound change that has occurred in all advanced industrial societies, including America, since the end of World War II. There is no going back to the old days (were they, indeed, as good as people of my generation remember them?) when most people got their political cognitive maps mainly from newspapers and magazines and from conversations with their families and friends.

Yet, the fact that there has been a profound and irreversible change in the way politics is presented and understood certainly does not mean that it has made our political and governmental system better. I am grateful to Richard Adler for calling my attention to a prophetic article published by Rudolf Arnheim in 1935, when television was still a laboratory curiosity. Arnheim saw the enormous potential of those flickering little pictures for becoming the pervasive transmitters of reality that in fact they have become. And, while he hailed the new medium's great potential for good, he also feared that television in every home might produce a "cult of sensory stimulation" by substituting simulated direct experience for the more demanding task of understanding by developing and improving concepts. He warned:

> Television is a new, hard test of our wisdom, If we succeed in mastering the new medium it will enrich us. But it can also put our minds to sleep. We must not forget that in the past the inability to transport immediate experience and to convey it to others made the use of language necessary and thus compelled the human mind to develop concepts. For in order to describe things one must draw the general from the specific; one must select, compare, think. When communication can be achieved by pointing with the finger, however, the mouth grows silent, the writing hand stops, and the mind shrinks.[16]

That seemed to Arnheim a real danger then, and it seems to me a real danger now. Even so, the ultimate impact of television on American politics or any other part of American life depends only to a degree upon what the networks' newspeople do. We can, I think, reasonably ask them to be more critical of themselves and more forthcoming with the rest of us about what they are doing and why. But, potent though television is and will remain, it is not and never will be the only powerful force shaping our society, our politics, and our visions of reality.

It therefore behooves the rest of us to profit from television's many benefits, criticize its many failings, and, in our own ways of participating in American political life, do all that we can to preserve and renew those values and institutions that we believe have been dangerously weakened in the television age. Television may not be of much help in that effort, but it need not be an insurmountable barrier.

Notes

Chapter 1

1. For children's consumption of television, see Letty Cottin Pogrebin, *Growing Up Free: Raising Your Child in the 80s* (New York: McGraw-Hill Book Company, 1980), p. 393. For adults' consumption, see George Comstock, *Television in America* (Beverly Hills, Ca.: Sage Publications, 1980), pp. 32–33; and Doris Graber, *Mass Media and American Politics* (Washington, D.C.: Congressional Quarterly Press, 1980), pp. 2–3, 120.
2. Quoted in Robert Metz, *CBS: Reflections in a Bloodshot Eye* (New York: Signet Books, 1975), p. 352.
3. Quoted in ibid., p. 354.
4. David Halberstam, *The Powers That Be* (New York: Alfred A. Knopf, 1979), p. 514.
5. The concept of "cognitive maps" was first used by the psychologist E. C. Tolman in *Purposive Behavior in Animals and Men* (New York: Appleton-Century, 1932). Its most influential application to political behavior was made by Angus Campbell, Philip E. Converse, Warren E. Miller, and Donald E. Stokes, *The American Voter* (New York: John Wiley, 1960), pp. 42–43.
6. For a comprehensive and critical survey of the pre-television scholarly literature about how people developed their conceptions of political reality, see Sidney Kraus and Dennis Davis, *The Effects of Mass Communication on Political Behavior* (University Park, Pa.: Pennsylvania State University Press, 1978).
7. A comprehensive and influential summary of the findings of the early studies of political socialization was Herbert H. Hyman, *Political Socialization* (New York: The Free Press, 1959).
8. The main expositions of the "two-step flow" theory were Elihu Katz and Paul F. Lazarsfeld, *Personal Influence* (New York: The Free Press, 1955); and Paul F. Lazarsfeld, Bernard Berelson, and Hazel Gaudet, *The People's Choice*, 2d ed. (New York: Columbia University Press, 1948).
9. For detailed accounts of the swift growth of television in the 1950s and 1960s, see Robert T. Bower, *Television and the Public* (New York: Holt, Rinehard and Winston, 1973); Lee M. Mitchell, background paper in *With the Nation Watching* (Lexington, MA.: D. C. Heath and Company, 1979), pp. 25–30; and Richard Adler, "Understanding Television," in *Television as a Social Force: New Approaches to TV Criticism*, Douglass Cater and Richard Adler ed. (New York: Praeger Publishers, 1975), pp. 23–47.
10. *Statistical Abstract of the United States, 1979* (Washington, D.C.: Bureau of the Census, 1979), Table 986, p. 587.
11. Edwin Diamond, *The Tin Kazoo* (Cambridge, Ma.: MIT Press, 1975), p. 13.

Notes

12. Ibid.
13. Ibid., p. 24.
14. Reported in Comstock, *Television in America*, p. 29.
15. David Littlejohn, "Communicating Ideas by Television," in *Television as a Social Force*, pp. 63-79, at p. 69.
16. Comstock, *Television in America*, pp. 125, 133.
17. Michael Schudson, "The Politics of Narrative Form: The Emergence of News Conventions in Print and Television," *Daedalus*, 111 (Fall 1982): 97-111, at p. 107.
18. Bower, *Television and the Public*, Table 4-4, p. 81.
19. Thomas E. Patterson, *The Mass Media Election: How Americans Choose Their President* (New York: Praeger Publishers, 1980), pp. 57-58.
20. Michael J. Robinson, "Television and American Politics, 1956-1976," *The Public Interest*, Summer 1977, pp. 3-39; and "American Political Legitimacy in an Era of Electronic Journalism: Reflections on the Evening News," in *Television as a Social Force*, pp. 97-139.
21. Edward Jay Epstein has shown that most viewers first choose a particular channel for their local news and leave the set tuned to that channel for whatever national newscast happens to follow. Hence the audience ratings of the national newscasts depend more on the popularity of their network affiliates' local newscasts than on their own efforts: *News from Nowhere* (New York: Random House Vintage Books, 1973), pp. 95-96.
22. Paul H. Weaver, "Newspaper News and Television News," in *Television as a Social Force*, pp. 81-94, at pp. 87-88.
23. See Evron M. Kirkpatrick, "Presidential Candidate 'Debates': What Can We Learn from 1960?," in *The Past and Future of Presidential Debates*, Austin Ranney, ed. (Washington, D.C.: American Enterprise Institute, 1979), pp. 1-50, at pp. 24-37.
24. Sig Mickelson, *The Electric Mirror* (New York: Dodd, Mead & Company, 1972), pp. 206-207.
25. Roan Conrad, "TV News and the 1976 Election: A Dialogue," *The Wilson Quarterly* (Spring 1977): 83-85, at p. 84.
26. Epstein, *News from Nowhere*, pp. 21-22.
27. See particularly Epstein, *News from Nowhere*, pp. 13-25; and Weaver, "Newspaper News and Television News," pp. 84-87.
28. Weaver, "Newspaper News and Television News," p. 86.
29. Epstein, *News from Nowhere*, p. 260.
30. Cf. Epstein, *News from Nowhere*, pp. 37, 150; Herbert J. Gans, *Deciding What's News* (New York: Random House Vintage Books, 1980), pp. 180-181; and Metz, *CBS: Reflections in a Bloodshot Eye*, pp. 357-358.
31. Daniel J. Boorstin, *The Image: A Guide to Pseudo-Events in America* (New York: Harper & Row, 1961); and Michael J. Robinson, "The Media in 1980: Was the Message the Message?," in *The American Elections of 1980*, ed. Austin Ranney (Washington, D.C.: American Enterprise Institute, 1981), pp. 171-211, esp. pp. 190-202.
32. Cf. Gans, *Deciding What's News*, pp. 122-123.
33. Epstein, *News from Nowhere*, pp. 133-134.
34. For fuller accounts, see Sidney Kraus, ed., *The Great Debates* (Bloomington, In.: Indiana University Press, 1962); and Kirkpatrick, "Presidential Candidate 'Debates': What Can We Learn from 1960?"

Notes

35. See Richard B. Cheney, "The 1976 Presidential Debates: A Republican Perspective," in *The Past and Future of Presidential Debates*, pp. 126–128.
36. Cf. Albert R. Hunt, "The Campaign and the Issues," in *The American Elections of 1980*, pp. 142–176, at pp. 166–171.
37. For a comprehensive survey of the strategic considerations in past and possible future debates, see Myles Martel, *Political Campaign Debates: Images, Strategies, and Tactics* (New York: Longman, 1983).
38. Dan Nimmo and James E. Combs, *Mediated Political Realities* (New York: Longman, Inc., 1983), pp. 2, 18.
39. Michael Novak, "Television Shapes the Soul," in *Television as a Social Force*, pp. 9–21, at p. 16.
40. Lee Thayer, "Communication—*Sine Qua Non* of the Behavioral Sciences," in *Vistas in Science*, ed. D. L. Arm (Albuquerque, NM: University of New Mexico Press, 1968), p. 54.

Chapter 2

1. For the circumstances and text of the speech, see William E. Porter, *Assault on the Media: The Nixon Years* (Ann Arbor, Mich.: University of Michigan Press, 1976), pp. 43–47, 255–262.
2. Doris A. Graber, *Mass Media and American Politics* (Washington, D.C.: Congressional Quarterly Press, 1980), p. 200.
3. *Facts on File*, November 13–20, 1969, pp. 745–746.
4. The point is made by many commentators. See, for example, Paul H. Weaver, "Newspaper News and Television News," in *Television as a Social Force: New Approaches to TV Criticism*, Douglass Cater and Richard Adler ed. (New York: Praeger Publishers, 1975), pp. 81–94; Herbert J. Gans, *Deciding What's News* (New York: Random House Vintage Books, 1980); and C. Richard Hofstetter, *Bias in the News* (Columbus, Ohio: Ohio State University Press, 1976).
5. Graber, *Mass Media and American Politics*, p. 272.
6. Edith Efron, *The News Twisters* (Los Angeles, Ca.: Nash Publishing Co., 1971).
7. Other leading exponents of the liberal-bias indictment are Joseph Keely, *The Left-Leaning Antenna: Political Bias in Television* (New Rochelle, N.Y.: Arlington House, 1971); and, on the specific topic of CBS-TV's coverage of the Vietnam War, Ernest W. Lefever, *TV and National Defense* (Chicago: Institute for American Strategy, 1974).
8. Efron, *The News Twisters*, pp. 50, 55.
9. Ibid., p. 207
10. Robert Cirino, *Don't Blame the People* (New York: Random House Vintage Books, 1972). Other works arguing that television news is biased in favor of conservative politicians and measures are Nicholas Johnson, *How to Talk Back to Your Television Set* (Boston: Atlantic-Little, Brown and Co., 1970); David L. Altheide, *Creating Reality: How TV News Distorts Events* (Beverly Hills, Ca.: Sage Publications, 1977); and Todd Gitlin, *The Whole World is Watching* (Berkeley: University of California Press, 1980).

Notes

11. Cirino, *Don't Blame the People*, p. 178.
12. Ibid., chap. 13.
13. Ibid., p. 2.
14. Paul H. Weaver, "Is Television News Biased?," *Public Interest* (Winter 1972): 57–74, at 66–67.
15. This view predominates among academic analysts of political television: in addition to Weaver, its main exponents are Edward Jay Epstein, *News from Nowhere* (New York: Random House Vintage Books, 1974) and *Between Fact and Fiction: The Problem of Journalism* (New York: Random House Vintage Books, 1975), pp. 199–209; Michael J. Robinson, "Television and American Politics, 1956–1976," *Public Interest* (Summer 1977): 3–39; Hofstetter, *Bias in the News;* and Michael J. Robinson and Margaret A. Sheehan, *Over the Wire and On TV: CBS and UPI in Campaign '80* (New York: Russell Sage Foundation, 1983), pp. 228–230.
16. An excellent introductory survey of television economics is Les Brown, *Televi$ion: The Business Behind the Box* (New York: Harcourt, Brace, Jovanovich, 1971).
17. Michael Mandelbaum, "Vietnam: The Television War," *Daedalus,* 111 (Fall 1982): 157–169, at 159–160.
18. Philip Geyelin in *American Media: Adequate or Not?* ed. Philip Geyelin and Douglass Cater (Washington, D.C.: American Enterprise Institute, 1970), pp. 12–13.
19. Edwin Diamond, *The Tin Kazoo* (Cambridge, Ma.: MIT Press, 1975), p. 63.
20. Cf. Graber, *Mass Media and American Politics*, p. 42.
21. For detailed discussions of the origins, meaning, and applications of "fairness doctrine," see Steven J. Simmons, *The Fairness Doctrine and the Media* (Berkeley, Ca.: University of California Press, 1978); and Henry Geller, *The Fairness Doctrine in Broadcasting* (Santa Monica, Ca.: The Rand Corporation, 1973).
22. FCC statement of 1949, quoted in Eugene S. Foster, *Understanding Broadcasting* (Reading, Ma.: Addison-Wesley Publishing Company, 1978), p. 322.
23. Epstein, *News from Nowhere*, pp. 226–227. See also George Comstock, *Television in America* (Beverly Hills, Ca.: Sage Publications, 1980), p. 45; and Michael J. Robinson, "American Political Legitimacy in an Era of Electronic Journalism: Reflections on the Evening News," in, *Television as a Social Force: New Approaches to TV Criticism*, Douglass Cater and Richard Adler, ed. (New York: Praeger Publishers, 1975), pp. 97–139, at p. 116.
24. Quoted in Robinson and Sheehan, *Over the Wire and On TV*, p. 61.
25. Cf. Epstein, *News from Nowhere*, pp. 205–227; John Johnstone, Edward Slawski, and William Bowman, *The Newspeople* (Urbana, Ill.: University of Illinois Press, 1976); and John Hohenberg, *The Professional Journalists*, 4th ed. (New York: Holt, Rinehart and Winston, 1978).
26. Epstein, *News from Nowhere*, pp. 210–211.
27. S. Robert Lichter and Stanley Rothman, "Media and Business Elites," *Public Opinion* (Oct./Nov. 1981): 42–46, 59–60.
28. Epstein, *News from Nowhere*, p. 214.
29. Gans, *Deciding What's News*, p. 211.
30. Richard Hofstadter, *The Age of Reform* (New York: Random House Vin-

Notes

tage Books, 1955). See also *The Progressive Era*, Louis L. Gould ed. (Syracuse, N.Y.: Syracuse University Press, 1974).

31. Gans, *Deciding What's News*, p. 205. See also David L. Paletz and Robert M. Entman, *Media-Power-Politics* (New York: The Free Press, 1981), p. 14.

32. Michael Jay Robinson, "Just How Liberal is the News? 1980 Revisited," *Public Opinion* (Feb./Mar. 1983): 55–60, at pp. 56, 59. For coverage in 1972, see Hofstetter, *Bias in the News*, passim.

33. Weaver, "Is Television News Biased?", p. 69.

34. Epstein, *News from Nowhere*, p. 217.

35. See, for example, Richard L. Rubin, *Press, Party, and Presidency* (New York: W. W. Norton & Company, 1981), pp. 52, 194, 199; Thomas E. Patterson and Robert D. McClure, *The Unseeing Eye* (New York: Putnam, 1976); and Dan Nimmo and James E. Combs, *Mediated Political Realities* (New York & London: Longman, 1983), chap. 2.

36. Thomas E. Patterson, *The Mass Media Election: How Americans Choose Their President* (New York: Praeger Publishers, 1980), esp. Table 3.1, p. 24. See also Robinson and Sheehan, *Over the Wire and On TV*, pp. 148–150.

37. For data on the relative media coverage of the early and late primaries in 1976, see Michael J. Robinson, "The TV Primaries," *Wilson Quarterly* (Spring 1977): 80–83.

38. Patterson, *The Mass Media Election*, p. 48. See also Comstock, *Television in America*, p. 67.

39. Epstein, *News from Nowhere*, p. 215.

40. Ibid., p. 216.

41. For example, such reforms as the new limits on the president's power to wage undeclared wars, the many changes in the Democratic party's rules for selecting national convention delegates, the proliferation of presidential primaries, the public funding of presidential nomination and election campaigns and the limits on campaign contributions and expenditures, the Freedom of Information Act, and the new conflict-of-interest laws governing appointments to federal offices.

42. For a recent exposition of this view by an ABC executive producer, see Av Westin, *Newswatch: How TV Decides the News* (New York: Simon and Schuster, 1983).

43. Thomas E. Cronin, "Looking for Leadership, 1980," *Public Opinion* (Feb./Mar. 1980): 14–20, at p. 17.

44. Robinson, "Television and American Politics, 1956–1976," pp. 19, 21. For a similar view, see Graber, *Mass Media and American Politics*, p. 199.

45. Quoted in William S. White, *The Taft Story* (New York: Harper & Brothers, Publishers, 1954), p. 89.

Chapter 3

1. Cf. Gabriel A. Almond and Sidney Verba, *The Civic Culture* (Boston: Little Brown and Company, 1966); and Donald J. Devine, *The Political Culture of the United States* (Boston: Little, Brown and Company, 1972).

Notes

2. Cf. Richard L. Rubin, *Press, Party, and Presidency* (New York: W. W. Norton and Company, 1981), pp. 148-149. (includes preceding two paragraphs)

3. The "CBS Morning News" has a higher proportion of political news to other material—and also by far the smallest audience—of the three network morning shows.

4. All three networks now follow ABC's lead in broadcasting some news programs between midnight and 3:00 a.m.

5. Edward Jay Epstein, *News from Nowhere* (New York: Random House Vintage Books, 1974), pp. 94-96.

6. Rubin, *Press, Party, and Presidency*, pp. 153-154.

7. National Opinion Research Center, General Social Survey for February-April, 1982, reported in *Public Opinion* (Oct./Nov. 1982): 28.

8. This general picture emerges from far too many studies to be listed here. The most comprehensive summary of the studies of the impact of television on people's perceptions and evaluations of politics is Sidney Kraus and Dennis Davis, *The Effects of Mass Communication on Political Behavior* (University Park, Pa.: Pennsylvania State University Press, 1976). A few of the best and most influential studies are: Angus Campbell, Philip E. Converse, Warren E. Miller, and Donald E. Stokes, *The American Voter* (New York: John Wiley, 1960); Campbell, Converse, Miller, and Stokes, *Elections and the Political Order* (New York: John Wiley, 1966); Norman H. Nie, Sidney Verba, and John R. Petrocik, *The Changing American Voter* (Cambridge, MA: Harvard University Press, 1976); William H. Flanigan and Nancy Zingale, *Political Behavior of the American Electorate*, 3d ed. (Boston: Allyn & Bacon, 1975); and Bruce A. Campbell, *The American Electorate* (New York: Holt, Rinehart and Winston, 1979).

9. Quoted in Edwin Diamond, *The Tin Kazoo* (Cambridge, Ma.: MIT Press, 1975), pp. 64-65.

10. Doris A. Graber, *Mass Media and American Politics* (Washington, D.C.: Congressional Quarterly Press, 1980), pp. 142, 143.

11. David Littlejohn, "Communicating Ideas by Television," in *Television as a Social Force: New Approaches to TV Criticism*, ed. Douglass Cater and Richard Adler (New York: Praeger Publishers, 1975), pp. 78-79.

12. It is worth recalling, in this regard, two well-known definitions of a "statesman": Harry S Truman defined the term as "a dead politician," and Eric Johnston defined it as "a politician who is held upright by equal pressures from all directions."

13. *Webster's New Collegiate Dictionary* (Springfield, MA.: G. & C. Merriam Company, 1975), p. 890.

14. *Roget's International Thesaurus*, 4th ed. rev. by Robert L. Chapman (New York: Thomas Y. Crowell Company, 1977), p. 594.

15. The Gallup poll, releases of July 12, 1973 and September 22, 1977.

16. Diamond, *The Tin Kazoo*, pp. 52-53.

17. See the discussion in chapter 2, pp. 31-63, of how television news typically portrays politics.

18. Michael J. Robinson, "American Political Legitimacy in an Era of Electronic Journalism: Reflections on the Evening News," in *Television as a Social Force*, pp. 97-139, at p. 101.

19. *Ibid.*, at pp. 113-114. For similar conclusions, see Graber, *Mass Media*

Notes

and *American Politics*, p. 187; and Michael J. Robinson and Margaret A. Sheehan, *Over the Wire and On TV: CBS and UPI in Campaign '80* (New York: Russell Sage Foundation, 1983), p. 261.

20. Kurt Lang and Gladys E. Lang, *Politics and Television* (New York: Quadrangle Books, 1968), p. 307.

21. The Harris Survey, release of November 25, 1982. The figures for the White House started at a low of 18 percent in 1973, rose as high as 37 percent in 1979, and fell back to 20 percent in 1982.

22. The literature on nonvoting is voluminous, but three of the most recent and useful studies are: Richard A. Brody, "The Puzzle of Political Participation in America," in *The New American Political System*, ed. Anthony King (Washington, D.C.: American Enterprise Institute, 1978), pp. 287-324; Raymond E. Wolfinger and Steven J. Rosenstone, *Who Votes?* (New Haven, Ct.: Yale University Press, 1980); and Ivor Crewe, "Electoral Participation," in *Democracy at the Polls*, ed. David Butler, Howard R. Penniman, and Austin Ranney, (Washington, D.C.: American Enterprise Institute, 1981), pp. 216–263.

23. Richard W. Boyd estimates that about one-quarter of the turnout decline has resulted from the "youthening" of the electorate: "Decline of U.S. Voter Turnout: Structural Explanations," *American Politics Quarterly*, 9 (April 1981): 138-150.

24. Cf. the summary in Paul R. Abramson, John H. Aldrich, and David W. Rohde, *Change and Continuity in the 1980 Elections* (Washington, D.C.: Congressional Quarterly Press, 1982), pp. 84–88.

25. For example, in 1982, forty-five states held both primary and general elections for one or more statewide officials. The average number per state was 8.5 officers elected in November. A voter in Texas faced choices for U.S. senator, U.S. representative, member of the Texas house, member of the Texas senate, governor, lieutenant governor, attorney general, treasurer, six high court judges, eight members of the state board of education, commissioner of agriculture, comptroller, commissioner of the general land office, and one railroad commissioner—a total of twenty-six races: *The Book of the States, 1982-1983* (Lexington, Ky.: The Council of State Governments, 1982), Table 7, pp. 108–109. In most cases the general elections were preceded by primary elections.

26. The story of the networks' development and use of sophisticated projection techniques and an account of the events on election night in 1980 are well told in Percy H. Tannenbaum and Leslie J. Kostrich, *Turned-On TV/Turned-Off Voters* (Beverly Hills, Ca. and Washington, D.C.: Sage Publications and the American Enterprise Institute, 1983), chap. II.

27. Notably in ibid.; and in *Early Election Returns and Projections Affecting the Electoral Process*, hearings held jointly before the Committee on House Administration and the Subcommittee on Telecommunications of the Committee on Telecommunications, Consumer Protection, and Finance of the Committee on Energy and Commerce, U.S. House of Representatives, June 10, June 29, and July 7, 1981, Serial No. 97–96 (Washington, D.C.: Government Printing Office, 1981).

28. Raymond E. Wolfinger and Peter Linquiti, "Tuning In and Turning Out," *Public Opinion* (Feb./Mar. 1981), 56–60.

29. John E. Jackson, "Election Night Reporting and Voter Turnout," *Ameri-

can Journal of Political Science (Nov. 1983, forthcoming).

30. The pros and cons of these and many other proposals are explored in depth in *Turned-On TV*, chaps. III–VIII.

31. Testimony of Elizabeth Byerly of the League of Women Voters of California, *Early Election Returns and Projections Affecting the Electoral Process*, p. 170.

32. In ibid., p. 8.

Chapter 4

1. To get something of the discussion's flavor, see a similar discussion in *Choosing Presidential Candidates: How Good Is the New Way?* (Washington, D.C.: American Enterprise Institute, 1980).

2. He was dismissed in early 1980 after Reagan's second-place finish in the Iowa caucuses.

3. William Cavala, "Changing the Rules Changes the Game: Party Reform and the 1972 California Delegation to the Democratic National Convention," *American Political Science Review*, 68 (March 1974): 27–44.

4. Cf. the summary, written in the mid-1950s, of American politicians' views about how to appeal to voters: Austin Ranney and Willmoore Kendall, *Democracy and the American Party System* (New York: Harcourt, Brace and Company, 1956; reprinted by the Greenwood Press, Westport, Conn. in 1974), pp. 342–344.

5. Kurt Lang and Gladys Lang, *Politics and Television* (Chicago: Quadrangle Books, 1968), pp. 301–302. For more evidence on this point, see Robert Agranoff, *The New Style in Election Campaigns*, 2nd ed. (Boston: Holbrook Press, 1976), pp. 261–266; and Doris A. Graber, *Mass Media and American Politics* (Washington, D.C.: Congressional Quarterly Press, 1980), pp. 162–163.

6. Larry J. Sabato, *The Rise of Political Consultants* (New York: Basic Books, 1981), p. 194.

7. Agranoff, *The New Style in Election Campaigns*, p. 269.

8. The most comprehensive account of the new political consultants is Sabato, *The Rise of Political Consultants*.

9. Anthony Smith, "Mass Communications," in *Democracy at the Polls*, ed. David Butler, Howard R. Penniman, and Austin Ranney (Washington, D.C.: American Enterprise Institute, 1981), pp. 173–195, at p. 177. For a similar view, see Thomas Patterson, "The Miscast Institution: The Press in Presidential Politics," *Public Opinion* (June/July 1980): 46–51.

10. For a survey of the direct primary in comparison with other candidate selection systems, see Austin Ranney, "Candidate Selection," in *Democracy at the Polls*, pp. 75–106.

11. See, for example, the assessments in Austin Ranney, *Curing the Mischiefs of Faction: Party Reform in America* (Berkeley, Los Angeles, and London: University of California Press, 1975); Samuel J. Eldersveld, *Political Parties in American Society* (New York: Basic Books, 1982), pp. 228–230; and Frank J.

Notes

Sorauf, *Party Politics in America*, 3d ed. (Boston: Little, Brown and Company, 1976), pp. 229–233.

12. Cf. Thomas Patterson, *The Mass Media Election: How Americans Choose Their President* (New York: Praeger Publishers, 1980), pp. 7, 116–117; William R. Keech and Donald R. Matthews, *The Party's Choice* (Washington, D.C.: The Brookings Institution, 1976), pp. 223–225; and Donald R. Matthews, "Winnowing," in *Race for the Presidency*, ed. James David Barber (Englewood Cliffs, N.J.: Prentice-Hall, 1978), chap.3.

13. In 1980, for example, one primary (New Hampshire) was held in February, nine in March, four in April, thirteen in May, and eight in June.

14. Michael J. Robinson, "The TV Primaries," *The Wilson Quarterly* (Spring 1977): 80–83 at 80–81.

15. The account in the text draws heavily from Austin Ranney "Momentum and the Media in Presidential Nominations," a paper presented at the Conference on Presidential Nominations, Dartmouth College, February 18, 1980.

16. The best accounts of Carter's drive for the 1976 nomination are: Elizabeth Drew, *American Journal: The Events of 1976* (New York: Random House, 1977); and Jules Witcover, *Marathon* (New York: New American Library, 1977).

17. Cf. Patterson, *The Mass Media Election*, pp. 126–128; and Richard L. Rubin, *Press, Party, and Presidency* (New York: W.W. Norton & Company, 1981), pp. 199–200.

18. See Pat Cranston, "Political Convention Broadcasts: Their History and Influence," *Journalism Quarterly* 37 (Spring 1960): 186–194.

19. Willkie's nomination, and the role played in it by the mass media, is a fascinating story well told by Donald Bruce Johnson, *The Republican Party and Wendell Willkie* (Urbana, Ill.: University of Illinois Press, 1960).

20. *Time Magazine*, 28 July 1980, pp. 16–19.

21. George Comstock, *Television in America* (Beverly Hills, Ca.: Sage Publications, 1980), p. 59.

22. Marshall McLuhan, *Understanding Media: The Extensions of Man* (New York: New American Library, 1964), p. 36.

23. Ibid., p. 261.

24. Tony Schwartz, "The Inside of the Outside," in *The New Style in Election Campaigns*, pp. 344–358 at p. 345.

25. Perhaps Connally's failure is explained by applying the principle of an old joke: A pet food manufacturer developed a new dog food, made according to the best principles of nutritional science, packaged attractively, and marketed with maximum media exposure, motivational advertising, and all the best techniques of modern marketing. But the product hardly sold at all, and the company's vice-presidents were at a loss to explain why. Finally the chairman of the board took some home over the weekend to try on his dogs. When he returned on Monday, he said he found the answer: "Dogs don't like it."

26. The most comprehensive recent survey of studies bearing on the point, by Eldersveld, *Political Parties in American Society*, chap. 16, concludes that the parties have in fact had more impact on government policy than is ordinarily said in textbooks.

27. The textbooks I have in mind were: V. O. Key, Jr., *Politics, Parties and Pressure Groups*, 5th ed. (New York: Thomas Y. Crowell Co., 1964); Howard R. Penniman, *Sait's American Parties and Elections*, 4th ed. (New York: Apple-

ton-Century-Crofts, 1948); Peter H. Odegard and E. Allen Helms, *American Politics* (New York: Harper and Brothers, 1947); and Charles F. Merriam and Harold F. Gosnell, *The American Party System*, 4th ed. (New York: Macmillan, 1949).

28. The classic exposition of the nature and fundamental importance of party identification is Angus Campbell, Philip E. Converse, Warren E. Miller, and Donald E. Stokes, *The American Voter* (New York: John Wiley, 1960).

29. The classic exposition of this view is E. E. Schattschneider, *Party Government* (New York: Rinehart & Company, 1942).

30. The classic expositions of this view were: Henry Jones Ford, *The Rise and Growth of American Politics* (New York: Macmillan, 1898); E. Pendleton Herring, *The Politics of Democracy* (New York: Rinehart & Company, 1940); and Herbert Agar, *The Price of Union* (Boston: Houghton Mifflin Company, 1950).

31. Leading statements of this view include: David S. Broder, *The Party's Over* (New York: Harper & Row, 1971); Walter Dean Burnham, *Critical Elections and the Mainsprings of American Politics* (New York: W. W. Norton & Company, 1970); Jeane J. Kirkpatrick, *Dismantling the Parties* (Washington, D.C.: American Enterprise Institute, 1978); Everett Carll Ladd, Jr., *Where Have All the Voters Gone? The Fracturing of America's Political Parties* (New York: W. W. Norton & Company, 1978); and Austin Ranney, "The Political Parties: Reform and Decline," in *The New American Political System*, ed. Anthony King (Washington, D.C.: American Enterprise Institute, 1978), pp. 213-248.

32. Meg Greenfield, "Thinking Small," *Washington Post*, 19 April 1978, p. A13.

33. See, for example, John F. Bibby, "Party Renewal in the National Republican Party," in *Party Renewal in America*, ed. Gerald M. Pomper (New York: Praeger Publishers, 1980), pp. 102-115; and Charles E. Longley, "National Party Renewal," in *Party Renewal in America*, pp. 69-86.

34. Michael J. Malbin, "The Conventions, Platforms, and Issue Activists," in *The American Elections of 1980*, ed. Austin Ranney (Washington, D.C.: American Enterprise Institute, 1981), pp. 99-141.

35. See Ranney, "The Political Parties: Reform and Decline;" and Kirkpatrick, *Dismantling the Parties*. We should note, in passing, that in 1982 the Democratic National Committee, acting on the recommendations of a new reform commission (the fourth since 1969) chaired by Governor James B. Hunt, Jr. of North Carolina, adopted several "reforms of the reforms," most notably a new rule setting aside about 14 percent of the delegate slots at the 1984 convention for the parties' governors, U.S. senators, U.S. representatives, and other leaders, and another new rule allowing state parties to avoid strict proportional representation of presidential preferences in allocating delegates: see Rhodes Cook, "'Superdelegates' May Pick Next Democratic Nominee," *Congressional Quarterly Weekly Report*, January 23, 1982, pp. 127-128.

36. Ranney, *The American Elections of 1980*, Appendix E, p. 369.

37. Cf. Robert J. Keefe, "Presidential Campaign Strategy Under the Law," Richard B. Cheney, "The Law's Impact on Presidential and Congressional Election Campaigns," and Michael J. Malbin, "Of Mountains and Molehills: PACs, Campaigns, and Public Policy," in *Parties, Interest Groups, and Campaign Finance Laws*, ed. Michael J. Malbin (Washington, D.C.: American Enterprise Institute, 1980), pp. 233-237, 238-248, 152-210.

Notes

38. Nelson W. Polsby and Aaron Wildavsky, *Presidential Elections*, 5th ed. (New York: Charles Scribner's Sons, 1980), pp. 22-23, 215-218, 285-286. See also Jeane Kirkpatrick, *The New Presidential Elite* (New York: Russell Sage Foundation and The Twentieth Century Fund, 1976), *passim*.

39. Cf. Graber, *Mass Media and American Politics*, pp. 157-158.

40. This argument is made by, among others, Richard L. Rubin, *Press, Party, and Presidency*, pp. 181, 230-231.

41. Sabato, *The Rise of Political Consultants*, p. 288.

42. I myself heard Jimmy Carter, in an informal White House talk to members of the Democratic party's third (Winograd) reform commission, say that of all the aspects of his campaign for the nomination in 1976, the one of which he was most proud was the fact that he owed nothing to any party leader or organization or special interest group and everything to the ordinary people who had supported him in the primaries.

43. Smith, "Mass Communications," p. 178.

44. Quoted in Kurt and Gladys Lang, *Politics and Television*, p. 80.

45. Sabato, *The Rise of Political Consultants*, p. 154.

46. Ibid., pp. 131-132. For other examples of gimmicks, see ibid., pp. 144, 154, 193-194.

47. Patterson, *The Mass Media Election*, pp. 21-25, especially Table 3.1, p. 24.

48. Quoted in Sabato, *The Rise of Political Consultants*, p. 153. Sabato adds, "When political advertisements are as trivial, at least there is usually a musical accompaniment."

49. Quoted in Harvey Shapiro, "A Conversation with Jimmy Carter," *New York Times Book Review*, 19 June 1977.

50. *The United States Government Manual 1981/82* (Washington, D.C.: Office of the Federal Register, National Archives and Records Service, General Services Administration, 1981).

51. Michael J. Robinson, "Three Faces of Congressional Media," in *The New Congress*, Thomas E. Mann and Norman J. Ornstein, ed., (Washington, D.C.: American Enterprise Institute, 1981), pp. 55-96, at pp. 62-68.

52. The point is made in detail by Edward Jay Epstein, *News from Nowhere* (New York: Random House Vintage Books, 1973), pp. 30-32.

53. A useful, though brief, discussion is presented in William J. Small, *Political Power and the Press* (New York: W. W. Norton & Company, 1972), pp. 162-165.

54. See the account by Edward Jay Epstein, *Between Fact and Fiction: The Problem of Journalism* (New York: Random House Vintage Books, 1975), pp. 78-100.

55. *Washington Post*, 19 February 1982, pp. A1, A14.

56. *Washington Post*, 27 April 1982, p. A4.

57. The quotations of Nixon and the other presidents are in Joel Garreau, "Up to Their Keisters in Leaks," *Washington Post*, 16 January 1983, p. B5.

193

Notes

Chapter 5

1. For a review of this remarkably consistent record, one of the closest approximations there is to an "iron law" of American politics, see Barbara Hinckley, "Interpreting House Midterm Elections: Toward a Measurement of the In-Party's 'Expected' Loss of Seats," *American Political Science Review* 61 (September 1967): 694–700; Edward R. Tufte, "Determinants of the Outcomes of Midterm Congressional Elections," *American Political Science Review* 69 (September 1975): 812–826; and Thomas E. Mann and Norman J. Ornstein, eds., *The American Elections of 1982* (Washington, D.C.: American Enterprise Institute, 1983).

2. Ivor Crewe's recent survey of election schedules in twenty-two democratic nations shows that the average period of time between elections for all of them is forty-one months. It is 40.6 months in Great Britain and, shortest of all by far, 24 months in the United States: in David Butler, Howard R. Penniman, and Austin Ranney, eds., *Democracy at the Polls* (Washington, D.C.: American Enterprise Institute, 1981), Table 1–2, pp. 226–229.

3. My discussion of this phenomenon borrows heavily from "Media Economic Indicators," a transcribed discussion held at the American Enterprise Institute on March 4, 1982, organized by newspaper columnist Nick Thimmesch and participated in by, among others, Herbert Stein, former chairman of the Council of Economic Advisors; Janet Norwood, commissioner of the Bureau of Labor Statistics; George Herman, economic corespondent for CBS News; and Jonathan Frobinger, economic correspondent for the *New York Times*.

4. The three quotations are taken from "Media Economic Indicators," pp. 5–6, 22–23, 34.

5. *Washington Post*, 18 March 1982, p. A1.

6. *Washington Post*, 26 November 1982, p. A1.

7. Quoted in Michael Mandelbaum, "Vietnam: The Television War," *Daedalus* 111 (Fall 1982): 157–169, at 157.

8. For two such analyses of the role of television in ending the Vietnam War, see Peter Braestrup, *Big Story*, 2 vols. (Boulder, Colo.: Westview Press, 1977); and Guenter Lewy, *America in Vietnam* (New York: Oxford University Press, 1980). Michael Mandelbaum, in "Vietnam: The Television War," argues that the country's experience in the Korean War casts doubt on this interpretation. He points out that there was, in Korea just as in Vietnam, early popular enthusiasm and later popular disillusionment with the Korean War, but there was little or no live television coverage of the Korean War; so he doubts that television was as important in ending the Vietnam War as some have argued.

9. Both quotations about the Falkland Islands experience are from Leonard Downie, Jr., "How Britain Managed the News," *Washington Post*, 20 August 1982, p. A15. For a British account, see *The Economist*, 22 May 1982, pp. 37–38.

10. Cf. Ben J. Wattenberg, "Too Bad for Our Side: War is a Video Game," *Public Opinion* (Aug./Sept. 1982): 60.

11. For the various antipower and antiparty strains of American political culture, see Austin Ranney, *Curing the Mischiefs of Faction* (Berkeley, Ca.:

Notes

University of California Press, 1975); Donald J. Devine, *The Political Culture of the United States* (Boston: Little, Brown and Company, 1972); and Samuel P. Huntington, *American Politics: The Promise of Disharmony* (Cambridge, Ma.: The Belknap Press of Harvard University Press, 1981).

12. Quoted in John R. Howard, "The Flowering of the Hippie Movement," in *Participatory Democracy*, Terence E. Cook and Patrick M. Morgan, ed. (San Francisco, Ca.: Canfield Press, 1971), pp. 206-210, at p. 209.

13. The literature on the development and present key role of the presidency is vast; the works that bear most directly on the matters discussed here include: Edward S. Corwin, *The President: Office and Powers*, 4th ed. (New York: Oxford University Press, 1957); Marcus Cunliffe, *American Presidents and the Presidency* (New York: American Heritage Press/McGraw-Hill, 1972); Thomas E. Cronin, *The State of the Presidency* (Boston: Little, Brown and Co., 1975); and Richard M. Pious, *The American Presidency* (New York: Basic Books, 1979).

14. Michael Schudson, "The Politics of Narrative Form: The Emergence of News Conventions in Print and Television," *Daedalus* 111 (Fall 1982): 97-111, at 102. For an illuminating inside account of the intensity of television news coverage of the presidency, see Judy Woodruff with Kathleen Maxa, *This Is Judy Woodruff at the White House* (Reading, Ma.: Addison-Wesley Publishing Co., 1982).

15. Pious, *The American Presidency*, p. 417.

16. Political scientists specializing in Congress have done some of the best work in the discipline, and I cannot list every work I have found useful. The brief account in the text is drawn especially from Richard F. Fenno, Jr., *Congressmen in Committees* (Boston: Little, Brown and Co., 1973); Fenno, *Home Style: House Members in Their Districts* (Boston: Little, Brown and Co., 1978); Ralph K. Huitt and Robert L. Peabody, *Congress: Two Decades of Analysis* (New York: Harper & Row, 1969); Donald R. Matthews, *U.S. Senators and Their World* (Chapel Hill, N.C.: University of North Carolina Press, 1960); David R. Mayhew, *Congress: The Electoral Connection* (New Haven, Conn.: Yale University Press, 1974); Randall B. Ripley, *Congress: Process and Policy* (New York: W. W. Norton and Company, 1975); and *The New Congress* Thomas E. Mann and Norman J. Ornstein, ed., (Washington, D.C.: American Enterprise Institute, 1981).

17. Norman J. Ornstein, "The Open Congress Meets the President," in *Both Ends of the Avenue*, Anthony King, ed. (Washington, D.C.: American Enterprise Institute, 1983), pp. 185-211. My discussion of television's impact on the Congress leans heavily on Ornstein's analysis.

18. Ibid., p. 189.
19. Ibid., p. 202.
20. Ibid., p. 205.
21. Ibid., p. 206.

22. Thomas E. Mann, "Elections and Change in Congress," in *The New Congress*, ed. Thomas E. Mann and Norman J. Ornstein (Washington, D.C.: American Enterprise Institute, 1981), pp. 32-54, at p. 37.

23. Quoted in Michael J. Robinson, "Three Faces of Congressional Media," in Mann and Ornstein, *The New Congress*, pp. 55-98, at p. 73.

24. Robinson, "Three Faces of Congressional Media," pp. 73-74, 80-82, 88-89.

Notes

25. Ibid., p. 94. (both quotations)
26. Ibid., p. 96.
27. Michael J. Malbin, *Unelected Representatives: Congressional Staff and the Future of Representative Government* (New York: Basic Books, 1980). My discussion leans heavily on Malbin's analysis.
28. Ibid., Tables A-2 and A-5, pp. 253, 256.
29. Ibid., pp. 4-5.
30. The literature on the quasi-independence of the bureaucracy from presidential direction is truly monumental. I have found especially useful: Chapter 7 in Pious, *The American Presidency*; Richard E. Neustadt, *Presidential Power* (New York: John Wiley, 1960); Louis Koenig, *The Invisible Presidency* (New York: Holt, Rinehart and Winston, 1966); Richard Rose, *Managing Presidential Objectives* (New York: The Free Press, 1976); and Hugh Heclo, *A Government of Strangers* (Washington, D.C.: The Brookings Institution, 1977).
31. From yet another enormous body of literature I have found especially useful: Anthony Downs, *Inside Bureaucracy* (Boston: Little, Brown and Co., 1967); Francis E. Rourke, *Bureaucracy, Politics, and Public Policy*, 2nd ed. (Boston: Little, Brown and Co., 1976); Harold Seidman, *Politics, Position, and Power* (New York: Oxford University Press, 1975); and Heclo, *A Government of Strangers*.

Chapter 6

1. Reported in the *Washington Post*, 5, January 1983, p. C10.
2. Cf. Percy H. Tannenbaum, *Turned-On TV/Turned-Off Voters* (Beverly Hills, CA and Washington, D.C.: Sage Publications and the American Enterprise Institute, 1983) Chapter VI; and statements by Dennis Leibowitz, vice-president and analyst of Donaldson, Lufkin, and Jenrette in Nick Timmesch, moderator, "The Telecommunications Age: We Are Already In It," panel discussion held on December 8, 1982, as part of the American Enterprise Institute's Public Policy Week discussions.
3. Ithiel de Sola Pool, "The Culture of Electronic Print," *Daedalus* 111 (Fall 1982): 17-31.
4. The estimates were made by Dennis Leibowitz and John Evans, executive vice-president of Arlington Telecommunications Corporation, in "The Telecommunications Age."
5. The reference is to Reich's book, *The Greening of America: The Coming of a New Consciousness and the Rebirth of a Future* (New York: Random House, 1970), which predicted that the counterculture revolution of the late 1960s would convert the ugly America of factories, greed, and pollution into a gentle land of communalism, cottage industries, and nature lovers.
6. Kas Kalba, "The Electronic Community: A New Environment for Television's Viewers and Critics," in *Television as a Social Force: New Approaches to TV Criticism*, ed. Douglass Cater and Richard Adler (New York: Praeger Publishers, 1975), pp. 141-163, at p. 151.
7. This caveat has been made by just about every analyst of mass political communications: see, for example, Joseph T. Klapper, *The Effects of Mass Com-*

Notes

munications (New York: The Free Press, 1960); *The Process and Effects of Mass Communications*, Wilbur Schramm and Donald F. Roberts, ed. rev. ed. (Urbana: University of Illinois Press, 1971); *Political Communication: Issues and Strategies for Research*, Steven H. Chaffee, ed. (Beverly Hills, CA: Sage Publications, 1975); and Sidney Kraus and Dennis Davis, *The Effects of Mass Communications on Political Behavior* (University Park, PA: Pennsylvania State University Press, 1976).

8. The first statement, by Howard Simons, managing editor of the *Washington Post*, and the second, by Dan Rather, Walter Cronkite's successor as anchorman of the "CBS Evening News," were made in the first broadcast of the series "The Constitution: That Delicate Balance," produced by Fred W. Friendly, former president of CBS News, and aired on PBS on January 5, 1983.

9. Walter Cronkite, "What It's Like to Broadcast News," *Saturday Review* 53 (December 12, 1971): 53–55.

10. See the summaries in Kraus and Dennis, *The Effects of Mass Communications on Political Behavior*, chaps. 3–6.

11. The most comprehensive scholarly study is Herbert J. Gans, *Deciding What's News* (New York: Random House Vintage Books, 1980).

12. Douglass Cater in *American Media: Adequate or Not?*, ed. Philip Geylin and Cater (Washington, D.C.: American Enterprise Institute, 1970), pp. 44–45.

13. Michael J. Robinson and Margaret A. Sheehan, *Over the Wire and On TV: CBS News and UPI in Campaign '80* (New York: Russell Sage Foundation, 1983), pp. 244–245.

14. See, for example, Colin Seymour-Ure, *The Political Impact of Mass Media* (London: Constable, 1974); Jay G. Blumler and Denis McQuail, *Television in Politics* (Chicago: University of Chicago Press, 1969); and Anthony Smith, *The Shadow in the Cave: The Broadcaster, His Audience, and the State* (Urbana: University of Illinois Press, 1974).

15. Anthony Smith, "Mass Communications," in *Democracy at the Polls*, David Butler, Howard R. Penniman, and Austin Ranney, ed., (Washington, D.C.: American Enterprise Institute, 1980), Table 8-1, at pp. 174–175. Time is given equally to all parties in Australia, Denmark, Finland, France, Japan, the Netherlands, and Turkey; it is given proportionally to the parties' voting strengths in Austria, Belgium, Canada, West Germany, Ireland, Italy, Spain, Sweden, Switzerland, and the United Kingdom. It is not given at all in India, Norway, Sri Lanka, and the United States.

16. Quoted in Richard Adler, "Understanding Television," in *Television as a Social Force*, pp. 23–47, at p. 28.

Index

ABC, 27–28, 66, 178, 179, 180; presidential campaign coverage by, 38, 83, 100
ABC News, 178
"ABC World News Tonight," 157
abortion, 51, 160, 165
Abscam scandal, 79
Adler, Richard, 181
advertising, 66; see also paid television (in campaigns)
affirmative action, 51
Agnew, Spiro T., 31–34, 37, 42
Agranoff, Robert, New Style in Election Campaigns, The, 91
Altheide, David, 40
Americans for Democratic Action, 52, 161
American Tobacco Institute, 49
Anderson, John, 26, 27
Antitrust prosecutions, 165
Arnheim, Rudolph, "Understanding Television," 181–82
Arterton, Christopher, 58
assassinations, 79
audience, see television audience

Bailey, Douglas, 92
balance of payments, 128
Bayh, Birch, 96, 97
Bay of Pigs invasion, 61
BBC, 134, 135
Berkeley Barb, 40
bias: in news programs, 34–35; in news reporting, 34; political, 35–42; against politicians, 58–60, 74–78; structural, 36, 42–62; in television coverage, 38–39, 41–42, 61, 118, 154
Boorstin, Daniel J., *Image: A Guide to Pseudo Events in America, The*, 22–23
Brinkley, David, 149
broadcasting, see radio; television
Brokaw, Tom, 100
Brown, Jerry, 97–98
bureaucracy, 151–52, 153–54, 155, 173
Bush, George, 26, 101
Byerly, Elizabeth, 85–86

Cabinet Council on Economic Affairs, 132
Cable News Network (CNN), 161–62
Cable-Satellite Public Affairs Network (C-SPAN), 161–62
cable television, 118, 158–60, 161–63
California primaries, 83–84, 98
campaign financing, 105, 107, 109–10
campaigns, 75, 80–82, 90–92, 113–16, 173; see also presidential campaigns; specific campaigns; television coverage of campaigns
Camp David accords, 119
Canada, 175
candidates, 101–3, 110–12, 114; see also individual entries
candidate selection, 92–94, 105, 107; see also campaigns; national conventions; primaries
Carrington, Peter (Lord), 119

199

Index

Carter, Jimmy, 120, 130, 141, 146, 175; *1976* campaign, 24, 62, 95, 96–99, 115–16; *1980* campaign, 26–27, 84
Cater, Douglass, *American Media: Adequate or Not?*, 176–77
caucuses, 57–58, 96–97; *see also* primaries
Cavala, William, "Changing the Rules Changes the Game: Party Reform and the 1972 California Delegation to the Democratic National Convention," 89
CBS, 19, 33, 177–78, 179, 180; presidential campaign coverage by, 15–16, 27, 38, 83, 100
"CBS Evening News," 52, 68, 69, 96, 157
CBS News, 46, 66–67, 86, 129, 142, 145
CCH, *see* Citizenship Clearing House
Center for Political Studies (University of Michigan), 76, 78
Chicago Tribune, 82
Chiles, Lawton, 114
Church, Frank, 97–98
Churchill, Randolph, 176
cigarette smoking, 49
Cirino, Robert, *Don't Blame the People*, 40–42, 50
Citizenship Clearing House (CCH), 75
Clark, Dick, 114, 152
CNN, *see* Cable News Network
cognitive maps, 6, 7, 29, 55, 58
Combs, James E., and Nimmo, Dan, *Mediated Political Reality*, 28–29
Commentary, 30
commercials, *see* advertising; paid television (in campaigns)
Commoner, Barry, 54
communication, 102–3, 164–65; message, 13–15, 165–66; "two-step flow" of, 7–8, 30; *see also* mass media
communicators, 14–16, 55–56, 65, 69, 100, 165; *see also* individual entries
Comstock, George, *Television in America*, 10, 11, 101

Congressional Quarterly Weekly Report, 81
congressmen, 117, 143, 144, 145, 148–50; *see also* individual entries
Connally, John, 103–4
Conrad, Roan, "TV News and the 1976 Election: A Dialogue," 17–18
Conservative party (British), 125, 126
conservatives (U.S.), 37, 50, 51–52, 54
Cooper, Frank (Sir), 135
Corman, James, 84
Council of Economic Advisors, 129
coverage, *see* television coverage
Cronin, Thomas, "Looking for Leadership, 1980," 62
Cronkite, Walter, 4–5, 46, 52, 96, 101, 134, 165; "What It's Like to Broadcast News," 168
C-SPAN, *see* Cable-Satellite Public Affairs Network

Daley, Richard J., 98
"Dallas," 177
Deardourff, John, 92
debates, *see* presidential candidate debates
democracy, direct, 160
Democratic National Committee, 108–9
Democratic national conventions, 98–99; *see also* individual candidates
Democratic party, 35, 62, 75, 125, 126, 179; delegate selection rules, 109; alleged media bias toward, 37–38, 39, 51; *1972* primaries, 95–96; *1976* primaries, 96–99; as possible cable TV operators, 161; *see also* individual politicians
Dewey, Thomas E., 82
Diamond, Edwin, *Tin Kazoo, The*, 9, 70–71, 75
Diggers (California group), 138
direct democracy, 160
direct satellite broadcasting, 158
Dole, Robert, 25
dollar, strength of, 126

200

Index

Dow Jones Industrial Average, 128
"Dukes of Hazzard, The," 177

Eastern Europe, 25
economic growth, 128
economic indexes, 128–29, 130–31
economic indicators, 128–31
editing, of news, 19–20, 21–22, 34, 47
Efron, Edith, *News Twisters, The*, 37–39, 42–43, 50
Eisenhower, Dwight D., 147
Eldersveld, Samuel J., *Political Parties in American Society*, 107
election night early projections of winners, 82–86, 95–96
elections, 173; *see also* presidential elections; U.S. congress: elections; voting turnout
electoral politics, 89–90
Ellsberg, Daniel, 119
Emmy awards, 62
Environmental Protection Agency: Office of Press Services, 117; Office of Public Awareness, 117
Epstein, Edward Jay, *News from Nowhere*, 18–19, 22, 23, 49, 56–57, 58–59, 67–68
"equal opportunities rule," 48
Equal Rights Amendment, 35
exit polls, 83, 84

"fairness doctrine," 48–50, 133
Falkland Islands War, 126, 134–35, 179
FCC, *see* Federal Communications Commission
Federal Communications Act, Section 315, 24, 28
Federal Communications Commission, 11, 24, 176; Broadcast Bureau, 34–35; "equal opportunities rule," 48; "fairness doctrine," 48–50, 133; news coverage requirements, 47–49; Office of Public Affairs, 117; programming complaints to, 34–35
Federal Election Campaign Act, 109–10

Federal Election Commission, 149
Federal Trade Commission: Office of Public Information, 117
Florida primary (1976), 97
Ford, Gerald R., 100–101, 141, 175; criticism by, of news reporting, 120, 130; *1976* campaign of, 24, 25–26, 115
forecasting, *see* election night early projections of winner
Fowler, Mark, 176
France, 175
free television time (in campaigns), 90–91, 93–94, 116

Gallup poll(s), 75
Gans, Herbert, *Deciding What's News*, 52, 53–54
Garth, David, 92
Geyelin, Philip, 45
Goldwater, Barry, 83, 144
Goodman, Bob, 111
Goodman, Julian, 33
"Good Morning, America," (ABC), 67, 145
Graber, Doris, 72
Graham, Bob, 114–15
Great Britain, 134–35, 175, 179; Foreign Secretary, 119; government of, compared to United States, 124–26; *see also* Falkland Islands War
Greenfield, Meg, "Thinking Small," 107–8
gross national product, 128

Haig, Alexander M., Jr., 119
Halberstam, David, *Powers That Be, The*, 5
"Happy Days," 162
Harris, Fred, 96, 97
Harris (Louis) polls, 75, 79
Herman, George, 129–30
Hofstadter, Richard, *Age of Reform, The*, 52–53
Hofstetter, C. Richard, 35–36, 54
Home Box Office, 158
Hoover, Herbert, 141

201

Index

"horse race" journalism, 57–58, 115, 127, 171
House Judiciary Committee, 167
House of Commons, 125
housing, 128
Humphrey, Hubert H., 37–38, 42, 98, 144
"Hunger in America" (CBS documentary), 19

inflation, 79, 125, 126
"Inside Story" (PBS series), 177
installment debt, 128
interest groups, see special-interest groups
interactive television, 159–60
interest rates, 79, 126
interviews, of journalists and politicians, 55–57, 59, 65, 100, 130, 145, 147
Iowa caucuses, 57–58, 96, 99
Iran hostage situation, 79

Jackson, Andrew, 139
Jackson, Henry, 95, 97
Jackson, John E., "Election Night Reporting and Voter Turnout," 85
Johnson, Lyndon B., 4–5, 24, 120, 133–34, 141, 144, 175
Johnson, Nicholas, 40
journalism, 65, 170, 171; "horse race," 57–58, 115, 127, 171
journalists, 17–18, 167–72, 174, 176, 178–80; adversary role of, 60–63, 122, 172, 179; background of, 38, 50–51; political beliefs of, 35, 51–54, 56–57, 58–62, 106; symbiotic relationship of, with politicians, 122; see also communicators; individual entries

Kalba, Kas, 162; "Electronic Community: A New Environment for Television's Viewers and Critics, The," 160

Kefauver, Estes, 144
Kennedy, Edward M., 26, 35, 52
Kennedy, John F., 15–16, 24, 51, 140–41, 144, 175
Kuralt, Charles, 19

Labour party, 125
Landon, Alfred M., 98–99
Lang, Kurt and Lang, Gladys, *Politics and Television*, 77–78, 90, 112–113
League of Women Voters, 24, 25, 27, 85–86
leaks (in government), see United States: government leaks
Leonard, William A., 86
liberals, 50, 51, 52, 54
Lichter, S. Robert, and Rothman, Stanley, "Media and Business Elites," 51–52
Lincoln, Abraham, 58
Linquiti, Peter, and Wolfinger, Raymond E., "Tuning In and Turning Out," 85
Littlejohn, David, "Communicating Ideas by Television," 9–10, 73–74

"M-1" (money supply), 128
MacDougall, Malcolm, 115
McGovern, George S., 95–96, 98
McLuhan, Marshall, *Understanding Media: The Extension of Man*, 102–3, 181
"MacNeil/Lehrer Report" (PBS), 157
magazines, 13, 22, 30; see also specific magazines
Maine caucus (1976), 96–97
Malbin, Michael J., "Conventions, Platforms, and Issue Activists, The," 108–9; *Unelected Representatives: Congressional Staff and the Future of Representative Government*, 151–52
Mandelbaum, Michael, "Vietnam: The Television War," 44–45
Mann, Thomas E., "Elections and Change in Congress," 149

Index

"M*A*S*H," 162
Massachusetts primary (1976), 97
mass media, 7, 102–3, 165; *see also* magazines; newspapers; radio; television
Mechling, Thomas, 114
medialities, 22–28; *see also* television coverage
message communication, 13–15, 165–66
Mickelson, Sig, *Electric Mirror, The*, 15–16
Miller, Warren E., "Misreading the Public Pulse," 78
Mississippi caucus (1976), 96–97
Mondale, Walter, 25
money supply, 128
Montana primary (1976), 98
Moral Majority, 161, 162
"Morning News" (CBS), 145
Moyers, Bill, 5
Mudd, Roger, 29
Murrow, Edward, R., 66
Muskie, Edmund, 95–96

Napolitan, Joe, 92, 111
Nashua affair, 26
Nation, The, 30
National Association of Broadcasters, 134
National Conservative Political Action Committee, 161
national conventions, 94, 98, 99–101, 105, 109, 112–13
National Organization for Women, 161
NBC, 56–57, 66, 84, 179, 180; presidential campaign coverage by, 27, 38, 100
NBC News, 178
"NBC News Overnight," 162
"NBC Nightly News," 52, 157
New Hampshire primaries, 26, 57–58, 95, 96, 97, 99; Nashua affair, 26
news, 17–18, 170–72; editing of, 19–20, 21–22, 34, 37; "scoops," 82; *see also* journalism

newscasters, *see* journalists
news gathering, 19–20, 21–22
newsmen, *see* journalists
newspapers, 7, 19–22, 34, 40, 68, 82, 92, 99, 112, 178; *see also* specific newspapers
news programming, news programs, 11–13, 18–19, 40–41, 68–69, 91, 157; bias in, 34–35; economic constraints on, 43–45, 66, 166; legal constraints on, 47–50; local, 12, 47–49, 67, 68; national, 12, 47–49, 67–69; time constraints on, 19–21, 45–47, 66, 67, 69, 73; viewers' trust in, 13–16
news reporting: bias in, 34
Newsweek, 22
New York primary (1976), 95, 97
New York Times, The, 22, 30, 37, 38, 46, 61, 112, 119, 142
Nielsen ratings, 9, 178
"Nightline" (ABC), 145
Nimmo, Dan, and Combs, James E., *Mediated Political Reality*, 28–29
Nixon, Richard M., 31, 129, 175; impeachment hearings of, 45, 144, 167; *1960* campaign of, 15–16, 24, 83; *1968* campaign of, 37–38, 42–43; *1972* campaign of, 85; and Watergate, 75, 120–21, 141, 167
Novak, Michael, "Television Shapes the Soul," 29

Oklahoma caucus (1976), 96–97
ombudsman, on newspapers, 178
opinion leaders, 7–8, 30
Ornstein, Norman J., "Open Congress Meets the President, The," 143–44, 145–47

paid television (in campaigns), 90, 91, 93, 115, 116, 166, 180
party identification, 105–7, 111–12
Patterson, Thomas E., *Mass Media Election: How Americans Choose Their President, The*, 12, 57–58, 115

203

Index

pay-television services, 158
PBS, *see* Public Broadcasting Service
Peabody award, 179
Pennsylvania primary (1976), 97
Pentagon papers, 119, 120
Pious, Richard, *American Presidency, The*, 142
Plante, Bill, 50
Playboy, 116
Poland gaffe (of Gerald Ford), 25
political advertising, *see* paid television (in campaigns)
political behavior, 6, 54, 65
political beliefs, 7, 13, 54, 64–65, 104–5; of journalists, 35, 51–54, 56–57, 58–62, 106
political bias, 35–42
political consultants, 91–92, 104–5, 111–12; *see also* individual entries
political culture, 64–65, 87
political information, 12, 30, 69, 71–72, 163, 169, 170–72
political interest groups, *see* special-interest groups
political maps, *see* cognitive maps
political organizations, 23, 87; *see also* individual entries
political parties, 105–10, 125, 147, 180; *see also* Democratic party; Republican party
political scandals, 79, 171, 173; *see also* Abscam; Watergate
political socialization, 7–8
politicians, 87, 116–17, 122, 168, 173; bias against, 58–60, 74–78; defined in *Roget's Thesaurus*, 74; defined in *Webster's Dictionary*, 74; *see also* candidates; congressmen; presidents; individual entries
politics: attitudes toward, 11–12, 64, 69–72, 77–79; as game, 55–57, 87, 89, 94, 113
polls, *see* public opinion polls
presidential campaigns, 56, 105, 107; (1968), 37–38, 42–43; (1976), 62, 115; (1980), 26, 27–28, 84, 85, 88, 100–101, 104
presidential candidates' debates, 28, 56; (1960), 15–16, 24, 66; (1976), 24–26; (1980), 24, 26–28, 70

presidential elections, 80, 127–28, 147; (1948), 82; (1960), 83; (1964), 83–84; (1968), 76; (1972), 54; (1976), 57–58, 95; (1980), 54, 57–58, 84; *see also* national conventions; primaries
"presidential vacuum," 152–54
presidents, 50, 139–42, 147–48, 152–53; Office of Communications, 117; *see also* individual entries
pressure groups, *see* special-interest groups
price indexes, 128, 129–30
primaries, 57–58, 83–84, 93–99, 104, 109; *see also* individual states
print journalism, *see* magazines; newspapers
Progressive movement, 52–53, 54, 89, 93
"pseudo-events," *see* medialities
public affairs programming, 11, 48, 65–66, 91
Public Broadcasting Service (PBS), 157, 177
publicity, *see* United States: public relations
public opinion polls, 5, 13, 25–26, 27–28, 70, 76, 78, 85, 137; *see also* exit polls; Gallup poll; Harris (Louis) polls; Roper Organization polls; television audience surveys
public policies, 123–24, 150–52, 164; *see also* United States: government programs
Pulitzer prizes, 62

"Qube" system, 159–60
quiz-show scandals, 11

radio, 15
radio broadcasting, 7, 99
Radio Corporation of America, 112; *see also* NBC
Rather, Dan, 29, 69, 168
ratings, *see* Nielsen ratings
Rayburn, Sam, 144

Index

reading (vs. television viewing), 12, 15, 70
Reagan, Ronald, 119–20, 124–26, 130, 131–33, 141, 146, 165, 166, 175; *1980* campaign, 26, 27–28, 84, 85, 88, 100–101, 104
Reese, Matt, 92
Reich, Charles, *Greening of America: The Coming of a New Consciousness and the Rebirth of a Future, The*, 159
Republican Congressional Campaign Committee, 108
Republican National Committee, 108–9
Republican national conventions, 98–99, 100–101
Republican party, 75, 99, 125, 126, 179; alleged media bias against, 37, 38; TV ads of, 166; TV channels predicted for, 161
Republican Senatorial Campaign Committee, 108
Rhode Island primary (1976), 98
Robinson, Michael J., "American Political Legitimacy in an Era of Electronic Journalism: Reflections on the Evening News," 76–77, 79; Robinson, Michael Jay, "Just How Liberal Is the News?" 54; "Media in 1980: Was the Message the Message?, The," 23; "Television and American Politics, 1956–1976," 12, 63; "Three Faces of Congressional Media," 117–18, 149–51; "TV Primaries, The," 95
Rolling Stone, 30
Roosevelt, Franklin D., 126
Roosevelt, Theodore, 140
Roper Organization polls, 13, 14
Rothman, Stanley: Lichter, S. Robert and, "Media and Business Elites," 51–52
Rubin, Richard, 65; *Press, Party, and Presidency*, 68

Sabato, Larry, *Rise of Political Consultants, The*, 91, 111, 114
Salant, Richard, 19, 46

Saudi Arabia, 119
Schudson, Michael, "Politics of Narrative Form: The Emergence of News Conventions in Print and Television, The," 11, 139–40
Schwartz, Tony, "Inside of the Outside, The," 103
"scoops," 82
Sears, John, 88–89, 113
Section *315*, *see* Federal Communications Act, Section *315*
"See It Now," (series), 66
Shriver, R. Sargent, 97
"$64,000 Question, The," 11
Smith, Anthony, "Mass Communications," 92, 112, 180
social costs, 115
South Carolina primary (1980), 104
South Dakota primary (1976), 98
Soviet Union, 25, 136
Speakes, Larry, 132–33
special-interest groups, 36, 106, 107–8, 161, 163–64
Spencer, Stuart, 92
Spock, Benjamin, 54
Squier, Robert, 114–15
Stanton, Frank, 33
Steffens, Lincoln, 53
Stein, Herbert, 129–30
structural bias, 36, 42–62
sunshine laws, 145
surveys, *see* television audience surveys

Taft, Robert Alphonso, 63
Tarbell, Ida, 53
telecommunications techniques, 157–58, 164
television, 14–15, 102–3, 165–67, 176–77, 181–82; interactive, 159–60; paid, in campaigns, 90, 91, 93, 115, 116, 166, 180
television audiences, 12–13, 68, 72, 77, 91, 156–57, 162, 165–66; *see also* television watching
television audience surveys, 9, 12, 44, 157

205

Index

television broadcasting, 7, 8, 38, 99–101, 158, 161–63, 179–80
television coverage, 22–23, 66, 118, 153–54, 166–67; bias in, 38–39, 41–42, 61, 118, 154; of campaigns, 80–81, 90–92, 93–94, 100–101, 127–28; of Falkland Islands War, 134–35, 179; of 1976 presidential campaign, 24–28, 95, 100; of 1980 presidential campaign, 94, 100–101, 114–16; of 1982 congressional campaign, 166; of Vietnam War, 4–5, 18, 31, 44–45, 134–35, 136, 177–78
television programming, 11, 40, 59–60, 157–58, 162, 177–78; public affairs, 11, 48, 65–66, 91; *see also* news reporting; specific programs; television coverage
television scandals, 11
television watching, 4, 8–10, 12–13; *see also* television audiences
Thatcher, Margaret, 124–26, 134–35
Thayer, Lee, "Communication—*Sine Qua Non* of the Behavioral Sciences," 30
Thurmond, Strom, 104
Tillson, John, 120
Time, 22, 30
time, as factor in politics, *see* news programming: time constraints on
"Today" show (NBC), 67, 145
Truman, Harry S, 82, 120
trust in government, 58–60, 74–79, 86–87, 174
trust in television news, 13–16, 18, 168
Turner, Ted, 161–62
TV Guide, 37
"Twenty Questions," 11
"20/20," (ABC), 177
"two-step flow of communication," 7–8, 30

United States, 136–37, 152–55; government leaks in, 118–21, 131, 132–33; government programs of, 51–52, 131–33, 166, 168, 174–75; implementation time of government programs, 74, 124–31, 173; President's Office of Communications, 117; public relations in, 116–18; public trust in government of, 78–79, 86–87, 174; *see also* specific presidents; U.S. Congress
U.S. Chamber of Commerce, 163
U.S. Congress: bureaucracy in, 151–52; as closed system, 142–44; elections, 80, 126–27, 148–50; 1982 elections, 125, 126, 148, 166; "mark-up sessions" in, 145; as open system, 144–47; party organization in, 143; press aides in, 117; seniority rule in, 143; televising of, 117–18, 145–47, 148, 149–51; trust in, 79; vulnerability of, 148; *see also* individual Senate and House committees, and members of Congress
U.S. Constitution, 33, 80, 137, 160; First Amendment, 33, 135, 176
U.S. Department of Defense: Office of Public Affairs, 117; Reagan rearmament-program study, 119–20; Vietnam War secret study, 119
U.S. Department of Labor: Office of Public Information, 117
U.S. Department of State: Bureau of Public Affairs, 117; Bureau of Security, 119; leaks in, 120
U.S. Supreme Court, 135, 149, 160; on newspaper's right to print information, 119; public trust in, 79
U.S. Surgeon-General, 49
University of Michigan Center for Political Studies, 76, 78
"Upstairs, Downstairs" (PBS), 60

Udall, Morris, 96, 97, 98
Ullman, Al, 84
unemployment, 126, 128

Vanderbilt, Arthur, 75
Variety, 52
videocassette recorders (VCRs), 158

Index

Vietnam War, coverage of, 4–5, 18, 31, 44–45, 133–34, 136, 144, 177–78; Tet offensive, 44–45, 134
"Viewpoint" (series), 177
Village Voice, 40
voters, 76, 83, 85–86, 125
voting turnout, 80–86

Walker, Dan, 114
Wallace, George C., 37, 97
Wall Street Journal, 22, 30
Walters, Barbara, 100
Warner Communications, 159
wars, *see* Falkland Islands War; Vietnam War

Washington Post, 22, 37, 45, 107–8, 119–20, 132
Watergate, 18, 45, 75, 120–21, 144, 167
Weaver, Paul, "Is Television News Biased?," 42–43, 55; "Newspaper News and Television News," 15, 20–21
Westmoreland, William, 177
Willkie, Wendell L., 99
wire services, 22, 41
Wisconsin primary (1976), 97
Wolfinger, Raymond E. and Linquiti, Peter, "Tuning In and Turning Out," 85
Woodruff, Judy, 100

207